HOLDING VALUES

What We Mean by Progressive Education

Essays by members of the
North Dakota Study Group

Edited by Brenda S. Engel with Anne C. Martin

HEINEMANN
Portsmouth, NH

Heinemann
A division of Reed Elsevier Inc.
361 Hanover Street
Portsmouth, NH 03801–3912
www.heinemann.com

Offices and agents throughout the world

The editors and publisher wish to thank those who have generously given permission to reprint borrowed material:

"Introduction" by Lillian Weber from *Roots of Open Education in America* edited by Ruth Dropkin and Arthur Tobier. Copyright © 1976 by Ruth Dropkin and Arthur Tobier. Reprinted by permission from the Workshop Center for Open Education.

Library of Congress Cataloging-in-Publication Data
Holding values : what we mean by progressive education / edited by Brenda S. Engel, Anne C. Martin.
    p. cm.
    Includes bibliographical references and index.
    ISBN 0-325-00724-1 (alk. paper)
    1. Progressive education—United States. 2. Education—Aims and objectives—United States. 3. Multicultural education—United States. I. Engel, Brenda S. II. Martin, Anne C. III. North Dakota Study Group on Evaluation.
LB41.H679 2005
370'.1—dc22   2004025129

Editor: Lois Bridges
Production: Elizabeth Valway
Cover design: Joni Doherty
Composition: Valerie Levy / Drawing Board Studios
Manufacturing: Steve Bernier

Printed in the United States of America on acid-free paper
09 08 07 06 05 DA 1 2 3 4 5

For Vito

Our beloved friend, our moral and intellectual lodestar

Contents

PART 6   RESEARCH AND EVALUATION

Introduction

BRENDA S. ENGEL

On a group of theories one can found a school, but on a group of val-
ues one can found a culture . . .

—IGNAZIO SILONE

I: History of the North Dakota Study Group

In November 1972, seventeen educators came together at the University of
North Dakota (UND) in Grand Forks to discuss a subject of crucial importance to their professional lives: assessment of student achievement. Those
individuals had been asked to meet because of their common interest in
equal access to good schooling—*good* in this case loosely defined as child-
centered, John Dewey-influenced, progressive educational practice.[1] The
persuasiveness and success of much of the work of the educators, in schools,
teacher centers, and institutions of higher education, depended on how student achievement was evaluated. At that time, and to some extent still, standardized testing with multiple-choice questions was not only the preferred
method but, in fact, the only method for assessing children's learning in
public institutions.

The meeting at UND was convoked by Vito Perrone, the dynamic, for-
ward-looking dean of the Center for Teaching and Learning at the University
of North Dakota. Perrone's purpose in bringing the group together was to
look with care at the current situation in evaluation and consider alternate
possibilities for the future. The issue was of particular significance because
the tests not only served to effectively define the curriculum—the lessons to
be learned—but also discounted much of the agenda of the more progressive programs. Schools that encouraged creativity, curiosity, and inventive
thinking, for example, were disadvantaged. Time spent on building a model
of an Egyptian pyramid, observing the patterns of growth in a tree, or painting a class mural was time lost in terms of standardized testing. Children in
progressive and "open" (also called informal) classrooms, although learning
perhaps with more depth and personal involvement, were not necessarily as
well prepared for tests as those in programs with more traditional methods

and content. For these reasons, published evaluation results worked against programs relying on inquiry learning and hands-on experience, giving them a bad name and at times threatening their ongoing existence.

As Deborah Meier pointed out in a pamphlet, "Reading Failure and the Tests" (1973), a child taught to think for himself or herself might well choose the wrong answer on a multiple-choice, standardized test. He or she would look for the answer that made sense in the context of his or her experience but not necessarily the one considered right by the test writers. One of Meier's examples shows a drawing of a woman holding to her chest a bag overloaded with groceries; she is facing a clerk who is weighing a bunch of bananas on a scale.

> Two children engaged in a verbal battle over the drawing of a lady shopping. "The man weighs the fruit before Mother buys it." [The correct answer] couldn't be right, according to one girl. "Where will Mother put the fruit he's weighing? She's already carrying one bag that is too full." Her classmate tried to demonstrate how Mother could carry another bag. The first girl remained unconvinced. (Meier 1973, 22)

Evaluation was a topic of intense concern for the educators gathered in Grand Forks; they felt that the dominant mode of assessing learning was narrow, dry, and often irrelevant to the aims of what they saw as good education. Some of them had just come from a much larger meeting of sponsors of the national Head Start and Follow Through programs in Denver, Colorado. Convened by the U.S. Office of Education (OE), the purpose of that meeting was to celebrate the accomplishments of the Follow Through program and to discuss its future. Its precursor, the federal Head Start program, provided (and still does) educational programs for poverty-level preschoolage children. Follow Through, funded somewhat later, was meant to extend the benefits of Head Start to children in kindergarten through grade three.

In 1972, there were almost two dozen operating models of Follow Through based on the pedagogical theories of the various sponsors, ranging from the educational right (the behaviorist theories of Bereiter and Engelman) to the left ("open education" influenced by contemporary British primary schooling). Each site had selected one or more from the list of sponsors to oversee theory-into-practice.

Perhaps for reasons of economy, Follow Through had been redesigned as an experimental rather than a service program like Head Start. The experiment, as conceived by the U.S. Office of Education, was to determine which of the models (and consequently sites) were most effective in educating children. Presumably the others would then be discontinued. The Office of Education had contracted with Stanford Research Institute (SRI) to identify the best models through standardized testing.

There was a strong presence of parents in Denver due to a Follow Through mandate giving parents an unusual measure of authority in the conduct of local programs. When the parents became aware, apparently for the first time, of the experimental nature of Follow Through and of the uncertain future of some of the sites, they became incensed. They were angered too by the Office of Education's explanation that the worth of the pedagogical models would be judged by standardized tests given to the children. The parents had little patience with Stanford Research Institute as a reliable arbiter and with test results as criteria of worth, and in fact with the federal Office of Education as an educational decision-making agency. They believed they knew more about the benefits of the programs to their children and resisted a narrowing down of recommended practices in early education.

The parents drew up a strong statement in full support of Follow Through: "We know that our children are learning. We know that they can learn. We have the evidence that they are learning and can learn. No one has ever asked us to demonstrate that Follow Through is working" (McDonald 1972, 12). In addition, "We are tired of others deciding when a program is 'not good' or 'good' for us, based upon their concept of 'data' and their concept of what is 'wrong' with our children" (McDonald 1972, 14). Parents demanded a voice in any future decisions on federal education programs with implications for their children and threatened to enlist the support of other parents nationwide. The Follow Through sponsors were quick to support their demands:

> One truth emerging from our experience in Follow Through is that the involvement of parents in decisions concerning their children is essential for effective education. Plans and counterplans that ignore this truth are unacceptable. (McDonald 1972, 15)

On this note, the OE-sponsored conference in Denver ended. Reliance on the results of the proposed SRI evaluation was abandoned. Parent power, which of course easily translates into political power in the form of votes, had effectively derailed the government's plan. A crucial question, however, continued to hang in the thin air of Denver: If not standardized testing, *then what?*

Vito Perrone was not present at the Denver meeting. However, some members of the group who met at his suggestion at UND came directly from the Denver meetings bringing with them insights and understandings gained at those stormy sessions. The seventeen individuals invited to Grand Forks were selected for a range of progressive values they held in common— on the content, process, and desired outcomes of schooling. Perrone's own institution, a Follow Through sponsor, was at the more progressive end of the continuum. Most present had already been in communication with each other—met, read each other's work, and visited each other's educational institutions. Their common enterprise had been the search for more constructive, relevant evaluation tools consistent with their beliefs about worthwhile educational practice.

The Early Education Research Group at Educational Testing Service (ETS) had previously done a report for one of the Follow Through sponsors—the Education Development Center in Newton, Massachusetts (Bussis and Chittenden 1970). The report analyzed the issues around evaluation and suggested some alternative possibilities. For the many individuals and institutions concerned with evaluation, this report defined the field, giving it a common language and common reference points. It also served to put these individuals and groups in touch with each other, thus incidentally preparing the ground for the future North Dakota Study Group.

> The report received a lot of attention from educators. But it never had much impact on evaluation practices of OE [the federal Office of Education]. I believe that Marjorie Martus of the Ford Foundation contacted us after she had read the report. I recall that Ford was providing support to the Workshop Center at City College and to a project of Ann Cook and Herb Mack, among others. This in turn led to meetings with Lillian Weber, Ann, and others. I don't remember when I first met Debbie [Meier]. . . . At any rate, I believe Ann Cook suggested to Vito that we be invited to the first NDSG meeting. (Edward A. Chittenden, personal communication, October 10, 2003)

Another theme of common interest among educators at the end of the sixties and the beginning of the seventies was the British primary school movement. American educators' knowledge of the movement was advanced by a series of widely read articles by Joseph Featherstone published in *The New Republic* in August and September of 1967. The articles, later gathered into a book (Featherstone 1971), described in detail the practices that had evolved in a number of English schools. They aroused great interest, particularly among more politically aware educators looking for teaching practices that would be consistent with a democratic ideology.

> There is nothing in England's placid political life to compare with the ferment in America over race, equality, and issues like community control. Nonetheless, visitors to scattered industrial and immigrant areas of Britain have noted large numbers of primary schools doing an exemplary job with the children of the poor and the working classes. England remains, like America, a caste-ridden capitalist nation; the millennium is far away. Yet, a comparable change in our schools would mean a great deal for the quality of our children's lives. (Featherstone 1971, xii)

Sparked by Featherstone's writings and by their own pilgrimages to England, some members of the American teaching establishment looked to the English *integrated day* as the model for the American *open classroom*. Among the teachers, schools, institutions, and teacher education agencies that were directly influenced by English practices were several of the Follow Through sites, including the one sponsored by UND.

Interest in English progressive primary education itself led to the development of networks of progressive educators. While working in the Brooklyn, New York, schools in the late sixties, Ann Cook and her husband, Herb Mack, encountered Vito Perrone at "one of those meetings" (Ann Cook, personal communication, June 2003). Recognizing their common interests and commitments, Cook and Mack subsequently went to visit the school of education at UND where Perrone was dean. As already noted, it was they who suggested some of the names of those Perrone invited to the meeting in Grand Forks.

That, then, is the background for the first meeting in Grand Forks, North Dakota. The original group members were energetic, experienced, and imaginative thinkers about schools and schooling and were professionally well prepared to take on the question: "If not standardized testing, then what?"[2] Vito Perrone opened the meeting:

> I'm really pleased that this many people were willing to come for a couple of days to deal with the issue of evaluation as it relates to more open processes of education. Evaluation is an issue that all of us have struggled with in a variety of ways over the past five to eight years. While some of what we have been doing is quite conventional, much of it breaks some fresh ground. Unfortunately many of the latter efforts in evaluation have not been disseminated very widely. Too much of what we are engaged in is being carried out in isolation. (1972)

All the individuals present had thought and written about school evaluation practices and had had practical experience developing alternatives to standardized testing at a variety of sites. Their purposes as a group soon expanded to include evaluation in traditional as well as progressive educational institutions. The need for better methods was seen as universal, not confined to one type of education.

A variety of alternatives were discussed, including new forms of testing, interviews, observations, longitudinal studies, checklists, collections of children's work, and program documentation. The conversation went on for three days, mostly focused on the intertwined subjects of documentation, evaluation, and reporting, although related subjects crept in among them: the role of parents, myths about education, and areas for research. At intervals, Perrone reminded the group of the urgency of the task at hand.

At the end of the three days, and after agreeing to keep in touch and meet again the next winter, participants dispersed to various parts of the country. In February 1973, most of the same group plus a few new interested persons met in Ida Noyes Hall at the University of Chicago. The same subjects were pursued with the addition of new information and news about progress. At the termination of that meeting, Perrone again asked (and continued for a time to ask at the close of each successive annual meeting): "Should we meet again?" Although the question was real, the response was never in doubt. After a few years, Perrone stopped asking. The group continued to meet over Presidents' Day weekends in February in conference centers in Minnesota, Massachusetts, North Dakota, Wisconsin, and Illinois.

As an anchor pulled up after many years on the bottom of a harbor brings with it long strands of attached material, the subject of educational evaluation necessarily brought into the spotlight many topics in education—all of them inextricably bound up with it. Over the years, the discussion broadened to include, among other matters of interest: early childhood education, the small schools movement, areas of the curriculum (e.g., art, science, literacy), second language speakers, John Dewey and other philosophers, Jean Piaget, Myles Horton, equity issues, educational standards, teacher education, teacher centers, racism, and cultural diversity. Consideration of these central issues in education—discussing, researching, writing about, organizing, and acting on them—constitutes the history of the North Dakota Study Group.

In the mid-seventies, the designation "North Dakota Study Group on Evaluation" (frequently shortened by omitting the last two words) was adopted by the participants. The title indicated the informal, voluntary nature of the organization, but also recognized its geographic origins on the Midwest plains, perhaps with overtones of both its plainness (no pun intended!) and its unlikeliness ("Why North Dakota?").

Although then a referable entity, the group continued in the same fashion—with no dues, no budget, and a mailing list instead of a formal membership list. Its continuing life was made possible by the efforts of Vito Perrone and his dedicated staff at the University of North Dakota and the energy created by the ideas and actions of the membership. The frustrations and misunderstandings experienced by this group of educators in their everyday professional lives and the felt pressures from a largely disagreeing education establishment also may have contributed to keeping the group together and ideologically coherent. Its strength, moreover, was continually reinforced by the developing warm personal as well as professional relationships among the participants.

The meetings themselves evolved into forums for the introduction and exploration of ideas, an opportunity to exchange references to events, people, and printed materials and to hear firsthand reports on the gains and losses in the never-ending struggle for worthwhile values and practices in education. Its function as an occasion for the reunion of like-minded friends and colleagues, however, was key to the group's longevity—and not separable from its intellectual and informative purposes.

Vito Perrone, the original convener, was the intellectual and emotional heart of the NDSG as well as its administrative center whether he was actually in North Dakota; at the Carnegie Foundation in Princeton, New Jersey; or at the Harvard Graduate School of Education in Cambridge, Massachusetts. The distinctive style of his opening and final summary remarks became not only annual expectations—part of the ritual—but key to the tone and content of the meetings.

Perrone's presentations were discursive, low-key, informed, often ironic, humorous, and inclusive. He summed up and interpreted what was happening on the national scene in education, putting it into a historical context (Perrone is a historian as well as educator). Despite his quiet tone there was never any doubt about the bent of his ideological and political commitments. His views were consistently guided by a vision of what he deemed good for children's learning, development, and general welfare. Something of Perrone's style, his gentle irony, can be felt in the following excerpt from his opening remarks on standards at the 1998 NDSG meeting.

> The standards-based reform direction is generally discussed as new to American education, getting us caught up with other major industrialized countries in the world. We should all exert caution every time we hear that something relating to schools is *new*. It usually means that those speaking of the new haven't chosen to examine the historical record. Our need for historical perspective is always large. Otherwise, we lose sight of the larger context, the roots of our work. We also lose, I believe, the potential for genuine reform. In addition, we should worry when the motivation to do something educationally is to help us catch up with some other country— a stance that seems to look right past the students most of us see day in and day out, almost as if they aren't there. I envision here a group of six- or seven-year-olds being told that they have to study hard to make sure we stay ahead of the Japanese. Why would any of these children care about competition with Japan? Why should their teachers even have that in mind? (Perrone 1998b, 7)

Vito Perrone's actual presence and gestures—his way of sitting back in his chair, taking his time, making eye contact with persons in the group— conveyed extraordinary warmth, openness, recognition, and appreciation of individuals and of the group as a whole. Deep seriousness and optimism-without-illusions, however, underlay his apparent ease and informality. He had a sophisticated understanding and knowledge of the workings of the institutional world and loci of power. His wide network of acquaintances in the field of education benefited the NDSG, bringing it additional members and speakers and greater visibility.

Until the mid-nineties, Perrone, as administrator, kept the mailing list and bank account; he obtained supportive grants and periodically requested donations when funds were running low; he oversaw the selection, editing, and production of a series of monographs published by the University of North Dakota under the imprint of the NDSG (see the listings of them at the end of this book). By keeping the administrative procedures largely in his own hands, Perrone was able to exercise quality control over the NDSG's output. He also influenced the Study Group's course of development: to continue as long as it proved useful and, as much as possible, to do so without the usual time- and energy-consuming organizational trappings. In a 1975 report to a funding agency, Perrone described the group with characteristic directness and simplicity, as "a relatively informal network of individuals with some common experience and with particular concerns about 'support systems for teachers' and 'evaluation'" (1975, 1).

As the NDSG continued, it began to develop a context of understandings and assumptions—a special in-group culture that, like all such cultures, had both strengths and weaknesses. Traditions established themselves—about procedures and rituals at the meetings, as well as often unspoken assumptions about values. Some of the positive traditions were, along with Perrone's opening introductory talk and final wrap-up summary, the inclusion of film, poetry, dance, and space reserved for individuals' special interests and passions. At the opening sessions, a ritual that members came to expect was an opportunity for anyone who volunteered to give a brief account of his or her current work, concerns, thoughts, or recommendations for reading or viewing.

Among the hazards were the potential for self-congratulation; easily obtained positive responses; and a sense of *specialness,* perceived at times as *exclusiveness,* particularly by newly attending participants. The NDSG membership's own commitment to democratic values generally served as a countervailing force working against thoughtless parochialism. People spoke out, often in painful ways, about unequal representation, authority, and voice. Classroom teachers and representatives of cultural and ethnic minorities at times felt slighted. In 1982, for example, a group of teachers from Philadelphia who were attending the meetings expressed their sense of being patronized—invited almost as "token" practitioners (from notes of telephone conversation with Lynne Strieb, March 10, 2004). Their voices and those of others began to be heard, their messages were usually acted on.

I was—and remain—puzzled as to my role and/or participation as a classroom teacher. Several years ago, some classroom teachers who attended the meeting decided that the NDSG was set up for educators who are not schoolteachers, and that this was all right. They felt that it provides teachers with a supportive network and resources, but did not need to have teachers attend the meetings. I am not sure that this is so. It seems to me that there should be a strong line of connection between the researchers/administrators/university people and the practitioners in the daily life of the classroom. (Anne Martin, personal communication to Vito Perrone, 1984)

It was not a coincidence that in the mid-eighties there was a distinct increase in the number of classroom teachers not only attending meetings but making presentations, serving on panels, and taking part in program planning.

A few years later the lack of leadership roles filled by educators from minority cultures was brought dramatically to the attention of the NDSG—the fact that African Americans and Latinos had come to meetings, mainly as invited speakers or as delegations from schools, but rarely returned. In 1986, Vito Perrone's interest in the National Coalition of Advocates for Students led him to invite Richard Gray, an African American then the organization's deputy director, to a meeting of the NDSG. Gray, along with Hubert Dyasi from the Workshop Center at CCNY and a number of other teachers and students brought the issue of minority involvement sharply to the attention of the group. They pointed out that it was not only a question of minority presence or leadership roles but also the urgency of establishing race itself as an ongoing subject for examination.

The minority students . . . as well as teachers . . . were very vocal [in] expressing notions of not just bringing in and sustaining minority participation in the group, but also about focusing on issues of race and equality in the annual meetings. . . . As you probably know, discussions of race have permeated most of the last several meetings. (Hubert Dyasi, personal communication, February 3, 2003)

The message, although painful, was heard and the situation began to change—more minority voices were heard and the leadership became more diverse (although there is still a ways to go). The NDSG continues to develop the capacity for self-examination and correction, surely one of the reasons members return.

Two months after the February 2000 meeting of the NDSG in Woodstock, Illinois, Vito Perrone suffered a massive stroke while working in his office at Harvard. Partially paralyzed and without speech, he had to suspend all activities including his leadership role in the group. Since that time, Vito Perrone has been fighting his way back toward a participatory life. He has regained a good deal of mobility, speech, and intellectual capacity and was able to attend the 2003 meetings held, for his convenience and in his honor, at the Harvard Graduate School of Education in Cambridge, Massachusetts. Other members of the group have taken on, at least temporarily, responsibilities formerly belonging to Perrone—communications, summary talks, and planning. But the central presence, the organization's heart, still remains mostly absent.

II: Values

> To lose a focus on democracy—not to be closely connected in our practice to the world, its problems, and its promise—is to lose the moral base of our work. (Perrone 1991a, 9)

Why the title of this book? What were the values held so tenaciously and articulately over the past three and a half decades by members of the NDSG? What were the intellectual shared territories and common purposes that lent urgency to the meetings?

First, a bit of relevant autobiography: I was born in New York City in January 1924, the same year Thomas Mann's *The Magic Mountain* was published. The novel, widely read—by my parents among others—concerns a man, Hans Castorp, who visits a friend at a tuberculosis sanatorium and ends up developing the disease himself and remaining there. The popularity of *The Magic Mountain* helped bring tuberculosis back to center stage for the educated middle class (where it had always been, of course, among poor and immigrant populations).

When I was five, I was taken to a prominent New York pediatrician who decided, on what later turned out to be flimsy evidence, that I had "potential" or "incipient" tuberculosis. My family panicked. I was immediately isolated and put to bed where, as far as I can remember, I remained most of the time for the next three years, cared for by a kindly woman, sent south for the cold winter months (Miami Beach, South Carolina), and totally isolated from my siblings and other children. At age eight, presumably cured of TB (although still sent early to bed and not allowed to exert myself), I was readmitted to the family and sent to school as a shy, illiterate, awkward child.

The Windward School, settled on by my parents, was a relatively unstructured and relaxed private school, probably considered suitable for the sensitive, delicate, inexperienced child I then was. Located in White Plains, New York (my family had moved to the suburbs), it was ideologically pure;

that is, pure John Dewey as interpreted by the somewhat naïve, semi-Bohemian, idealistic group of parents and teachers who had founded it not long before I was enrolled. The school shared most of the hallmarks of other progressive schools of the 1920s and 1930s: woodworking at the center of the curriculum (if indeed there was anything that could have been described as a curriculum); a great deal of time and importance given to art, crafts, and nature study; weekly field trips; lots of encouragement to invent and explore; project-based learning; teachers addressed by their first names; high parent involvement (it wasn't always clear to us who were the parents and who were the teachers); and an absence of textbooks. "Arithmetic" was the only subject taught in noninnovative ways—probably for lack of know-how—and it was the only subject we found boring.

I have intermittent and perhaps undependable memories of the school: a teacher, Kitty, who taught literature and theater—who was thought (by us children) to live on the stage and wear the costumes in daily life. (Or perhaps it was the reverse—the costumes for the plays were selected from her personal wardrobe.) We designed and constructed one of the school buildings and I learned to hammer nails, mix mortar, and lay bricks. I must also have learned to read though I don't remember much by way of process—except that I was introduced on the first day to a teacher named Marcelle and she apparently showed me how.

We studied medieval times through literature, history, and art; built a model of a medieval town; and visited a real castle with a stone-paved courtyard on the Whitelaw-Reid estate in upper Westchester County. We studied bridges and dams and made field trips to the George Washington Bridge and Kensico Dam. I spent a great deal of time in the art room drawing and painting. At the start of each week, we were given a "contract" to fill out specifying the work we meant to accomplish in those five days. My best friend usually completed her contract by Tuesday; as far as I remember, I never did complete one although it didn't seem to matter.

I loved the Windward School. Although my years there have undoubtedly been romanticized through selective memory, they seem to have been full of wonder, discovery, and pleasure. I went from being a distinctly strange, semi-invalid child to being an active learner, enthusiastic about school and education and curious about the wider world. One of the most important things we all learned at the school was a kind of confidence that we, by ourselves, could do it, make it, find out about it.

Many years later, visiting primary schools in England in 1969, I recognized with delight beliefs and practices from my own early experience of school (only there the schools were public and inclusive): value put on the arts and creative effort, trust in the implicit interest of the man-made and natural worlds, respect for children's autonomy, and belief in children's serious mindedness and serious intent. These, with the addition of belief in democratic community and inclusion, are the closest I can get to defining the *values* behind the work of the North Dakota Study Group. To have meaning, of course, they have to be in context, not merely appear on a checklist. They are distinctly different from those values held by the majority of the educational establishment that, with some notable exceptions, lie behind conduct of public education.

Since the days of excitement over the *integrated day* (the English version) and *open education* or *informal education* (the American translations), those terms, along with *progressive education* (from the work of John Dewey), have become suspect. Attaching them as descriptors to any educational endeavor brings considerable risk in the current political climate.

Dewey's own use of the word *progressive* was applied in fact more to society and politics than directly to education. He believed that "progressive communities . . . endeavor to shape the experiences of the young so that instead of reproducing current habits, better habits shall be formed, and thus the future adult society will be an improvement on their own" (Dewey 1944, 1916, 79). For John Dewey education was "an instrument of realizing the better hopes of men" (79); he went on to prescribe what such an education for change might be. (My understanding of John Dewey's philosophy of education has been deepened and extended by many conversations and exchanges of emails with George Hein, colleague and friend.)

Conservatives favor education as a *handing down* of values and academic content to each succeeding generation, with students seen primarily as receivers of knowledge rather than as active creators of meaning. The difference between the conservative and progressive positions could be characterized as maintaining the status quo versus moving forward. Neither view, of course, is monolithic and both depend on what kind of society or culture is envisaged for the future. Dewey stated this succinctly in 1916:

> Particularly is it true that a society which not only changes but which has the ideal of such change as will improve it, will have different standards and methods of education from one which aims simply at the perpetuation of its own customs. (81)

In recent years, the country has moved toward the right, politically and ideologically maintaining what is essentially a conservative ideology by Dewey's definition. Since public education is inevitably tied in with national and local politics, it too has moved toward the right. This means, on the school level, prescribed curriculum, standards imposed from above, and increased standardized testing—all justified by a rhetoric of rigor and economic necessity. These leave little room for the arts and imagination or inquiry learning.

Yet . . . yet . . . an undercurrent of progressive educational practices persists, and, even when not named or recognized as such, continues to influence schools in many ways. The evidence: instances of project-based learning; assessment by portfolio; hands-on activities; emphasis on inquiry, on small classes, and on small schools. The dissonance between, on the one hand, those schools and individual teachers trying to act on their own convictions about how and why children learn and, on the other hand, officials responsible for carrying out top-down policy decisions has led at times to political action, passive resistance, and even occasionally deception (like altering test scores).

Some of those attending the early meetings of the North Dakota Study Group were veterans of school battles—ideological and political struggles—and had been active in promoting equal access to good education for all children. Others were occupied primarily with developing progressive educational practice and child study. The ideology of the two activities coincided to a remarkable extent: the nature of practice and the policies that enable or hamper it are interdependent (though less so, of course, in independent schools). Vito Perrone himself was notably an effective progressive educator with a high degree of political awareness. And the galvanizing issue on the table in Grand Forks, evaluation, had immediate implication for both politics and education.

The issue of educational evaluation has to do basically with power relationships, which are at the heart of politics: Who has the right to evaluate what and whom? Who decides on criteria and instruments? What degree of consent needs to be sought from those having a stake in the consequences? Finally, there are the questions about values themselves—*what* values are lurking behind judgments? These questions lead to further questions: Can so-called "objective" methods determine the worth of qualitative experiences like education?

Michael Patton, at the time of the 1972 meeting still a graduate student in sociology at the University of Wisconsin, later wrote one of the first monographs published under the imprint of the North Dakota Study Group (1975). Proposing an alternative research paradigm for the fields of education and sociology, Patton contrasted characteristics of quantitative and qualitative methodologies: reliability versus validity, objectivity versus subjectivity, distance from versus closeness to the data, component analysis versus holistic, outcome versus process evaluation, generalization versus uniqueness. The second in each of these pairs is consonant with the beliefs and inclinations of members of the NDSG. Taken together, they describe not so much a political stance as a context for making decisions—one that assumes the importance of the individual's experience and views and emphasizes understanding over judgment.

Edward Chittenden and Anne Bussis and colleagues in the Early Education group of Educational Testing Service, in Princeton, New Jersey, mentioned in Part I of this introduction, were thinking in ways congenial with Patton's analysis. As psychologists and educational researchers, they developed qualitative ways of looking at children's learning, their methods relying on closeness to the subjects being studied with validity (relevance) established by detailed observation of children in the process of learning. They emphasized the importance of context—the particular group of children, particular teacher and particular setting—to academic outcomes. In planning a study of children learning to read, the ETS researchers spent a week at the Prospect School in Vermont consulting with Patricia Carini and colleagues who had been developing useful protocols for observing children. Bussis and Chittenden, with their coauthors Marianne Amarel and Edith Klausner, also spent time with children in classes—many of them taught by members of the NDSG.

> A research focus on readers carries several methodological consequences. It implies the need for evidence of a child's understandings and manner of functioning across the full range of classroom activities. It requires a study over time, in order that patterns may emerge from the documented evidence and the relationship of reading to the reader's broader purposes and meanings may be discerned. A focus on readers also calls for the in-depth study of relatively few learners rather than gathering more limited data on a great many children. It means, in effect, an approach using naturalistic methods and procedures that can be sustained over time. (Bussis, Chittenden, Amarel, and Klausner 1985, ix)

Aside from the study's close-up view, breadth, length, and emphasis on meaning, another striking (and unusual) characteristic of the ETS reading study was its collaborative design—researchers coequal with practitioners: "Practitioners were centrally involved in all phases of the investigation, from planning and instrument development through data collection and analysis" (1985, x).

The ETS team had deep respect for, in fact depended on, the knowledge, insights, and understanding of the classroom teachers. Unlike the stance of the Office of Education in Denver, they did not set themselves up as experts, deciding the criteria for judgment and anticipating the nature of the decisions that would be attendant on its outcomes. In seeking the collaboration of subjects, Bussis and colleagues were acting perhaps more for practical reasons than for political and/or ideological ones. Just as Willie Sutton robbed banks because, as he said, that was where the money was, the ETS researchers understood where the knowledge was: in children and teachers. Still it is striking that they consistently maintained "democratic" relationships with study subjects as well as within their own collaborative group at ETS.

In the mid-seventies, with my help, George Hein formed the Program Evaluation and Research Group (PERG) at Lesley College (now University) in Cambridge, Massachusetts. Its political and educational ideology was consistent with that of the NDSG, although it's difficult to know whether PERG was influenced by the beliefs of the NDSG or whether it was drawn to the NDSG in the first place because of already existing sympathies; it was probably a combination of both. In a 1977 monograph on evaluation, I wrote, "People have the right to participate as active agents in decisions that directly affect them" (Engel 1977, 3); and "Unity of thought and action leads toward freedom of the individual—whenever a person acts in obedience to someone else's thinking, he is giving up a measure of independence" (4).

Although these statements pertained to practices in evaluation, they were essentially political in nature, having to do with power and authority. The practices of PERG followed the guidelines of qualitative evaluation as described earlier by Michael Patton. Clients initially were asked to articulate their own goals and evaluation was conceived as a collaborative effort, its purpose to achieve deeper understanding in the service of program improvement. The instruments, too, were primarily qualitative: interviews, observations, questionnaires, collections of artifacts, and so on, although the results of some of these, particularly of the questionnaires, were frequently converted into numbers. Neither in its conduct nor purposes did PERG typify the *de haut en bas* assumptions of most evaluation practice. However, the PERG methods were not easily adapted, for some of the same reasons, to large-scale, national assessments. If it had been responsible for the Follow Through assessments, the sites would have been individually evaluated with the aims and perceptions of those immediately involved taken into account. Plus, the purpose would have been improvement of each site, not the kind of *horse race* designed by the Office of Education to determine the "best method."

Some educators who attended the first meeting in Grand Forks had a high level of political consciousness and experience. These included four from New York City: Lillian Weber, Deborah Meier, Ann Cook, and Herb Mack. Weber, the oldest and most experienced of the group, was professor of Early Childhood Education at the City College of New York and also director of Advisory Services to the Open Corridor Reorganization of the New York City public schools. Weber's basic commitment was to greater access for all children to good (i.e., progressive, child-centered) schooling, no matter what their age, class, or race. This meant, of course, public education. In the United States until that time, progressive education had been mostly limited to private (independent) schools. In the late sixties, Weber heard about the new primary school education, known as the integrated day, being practiced in some areas of England.

> It had not been clear to me that "good" education could exist under the conditions usually found in the public sector until I discovered that England had what I considered to be "good" education, even with large classes, and that it provided this in the state framework. (Weber 1971, 1)

Weber spent a year and a half in England studying British education and observing schools for young children. On her return she wrote a book describing in detail the creative, child-centered practices she had seen in state schools. Her interest had always been in bringing about change in the system of compulsory education in the United States. She saw the structures of American education as a mismatch with the nature of children—with children's innate ways of learning. Essentially a pragmatist, however, Weber was able to work within the givens, gradually creating developmental learning communities in classrooms grouped around an "open corridor." Children and teachers used the corridors for display and as alternative workspaces. Teachers began to see themselves as part of a community of peers rather than as individuals isolated in their classrooms. The corridors were *open* too in that they made the education community accessible to parents and other visitors. Moreover the curriculum itself made use of the surrounding culture rather than being confined strictly to academics.

Weber supported teachers' growth and change by instituting a system of "advisors," a model imported from England. The advisors were there to help and suggest rather than supervise in the traditional sense—again, a more democratic relationship instead of the usual vertical hierarchy of power and authority.

Deborah Meier was one of Lillian Weber's advisors in Districts Two and Three in New York City. A longtime socialist and political activist, Meier wrote several pamphlets criticizing standardized testing of reading. She also published articles in the teachers' union magazine, in *Dissent,* and in various other journals even though she saw herself primarily as a teacher:

> I certainly didn't see my political agenda as primary in my work in schools. I went into being a kindergarten teacher for the sheer fascination of it, quite surprisingly, although I always saw it as compatible with my politics and values. (Meier, personal communication, January 2, 2003)

Meier, like Lillian Weber, had visited England in the sixties, recognizing there some elements of the progressive pedagogy she herself had experienced as a child in private school. Again like Weber, she had a vision of bringing thoughtful, developmental, exciting education into the public domain.

The thrill of the English developments was that they were reaching working-class kids, ordinary schools and suggested to us the possibility that these ideas might be viable for more than the small, private school elite that was still influenced by Deweyism. (Meier 2003)

In 1974, Deborah Meier was asked by a district administrator to create a new public school in New York City's District 4 where a system of school choice had recently been instituted. Central Park East (CPE) in East Harlem, the school Meier started, was (and still is) an outstanding example of a distinctive, innovative, and successful learning community. Although attended by a diverse body of students as in other public schools, CPE was very different in its pedagogy and explicit values. The school, with a relatively small total enrollment, was characterized by small classes, project-based curriculum, centrality of the arts, developmental learning theory, and a good deal of teacher autonomy. Guiding these practices were strong convictions about educating for a democratic society: That children—all human beings in fact—are capable of making responsible choices, being engaged by the things of this world, asking good questions, and becoming independent thinkers and learners.

Respect for the dignity and worth of the individual student worked against practices such as tracking, conventional grading, and standardized testing—all of which are associated with top-down judgments. Motivation for learning came in part from the close association of adults and children (adults serving as "models" of readers, artists, scientists, and engaged thinkers) and from the surrounding natural and man-made worlds viewed as an always-intriguing subject for exploration.

Although Ann Cook and Herb Mack also created a public school in New York City, they had originally come to education from a background of political activism. Cook, while still a student at Sarah Lawrence College, helped organize a national conference on civil rights. Later, in the early sixties in Chicago, she and Mack, then a high school teacher, initiated a program in which high schoolers were tutored by college students (SWAT). Both Cook and Mack were involved in a number of civil rights organizations (including the Student Non-Violent Coordinating Committee) and public actions (boycotts, freedom schools). In 1966, they too traveled to England where they stayed and worked for two years, interested in the new ideas and practices they found there. Their initial focus was attitudes toward race in state comprehensive schools though while there they also participated in projects on curriculum development.

Back in the United States, during the period of administrative decentralization in New York City, Cook and Mack worked with the city's public schools and, in the early seventies, established the Community Resources

Institute. The institute, similar to the English advisories, provided material resources, workshops, and consultation for teachers. In 1985, they founded the Urban Academy, a small New York City public high school.

Ann Cook and Herb Mack, like Deborah Meier and Lillian Weber, have stood for—and fought for—progressive values in education, ones that they saw as compatible with their political ideology: respect for and confidence in the individual learner, antiracism, creative curriculum related to students' experience with the outside world, and education for participation in the community and in a democratic society.

During the period when Weber, Meier, Cook, and Mack were creating or influencing educational institutions in New York, Patricia Carini co-founded, in 1965, a small, independent, "alternative" elementary school in southern Vermont. At the 1972 meeting in Grand Forks, Carini was an articulate, passionate speaker. Her experience and development of documentary processes at the Prospect School offered promise for responding to the question, "If not standardized testing, then what?"

Teaching practices at the Prospect School were influenced by the examples of primary school education in England as well as by John Dewey and the traditions of progressive education in the United States. But the school—staff and administrators—also developed its own pedagogy and practice from seeing, experiencing, reflecting, and discussing, and from broad reading; philosophy and psychology, educational theory, poetry, and fiction.

> [The school] reflects a humanistic understanding of how children learn: through play they follow their natural curiosity to explore the world and their relation to it; through science, language and art they learn to represent, describe and express their continually evolving perceptions of the world; through firsthand involvement they seek and extend their individual interests and personal meanings. (Prospect School Brochure, n.d.).

Carini herself, in addition to being an educator, is a philosopher, psychologist, avid reader, and creative thinker. She has developed, with the school's teachers, ways of observing and recording children's in-school lives in order to gain deeper understanding of who they, the children, are as learners and creators of meaning—in her words, making them "visible."

Carini's essentially nonjudgmental, descriptive, and appreciative approach to deeper understanding of children depends on extensive documentation: observations by teachers and administrators, collections of children's work, interviews—all qualitative data. The view, in Patton's terms, was of "closeness to the data." Documentation served as material for staff "reflections" aimed at providing for children's interests, propensities, and ways of learning. The "Prospect Processes," as they came to be called, were a new form of evaluation in the service of supporting the child's full development rather than judging mainly academic achievement.

> I first heard of Patricia Carini and the Prospect School in 1971 when I faced the task of evaluating a new, alternative school. It was immediately evident to me, from what I heard and read, that Carini was thinking about children and education in ways [that] were both startlingly original and, at the same time, had a distinct ring of truth. I made arrangements to spend ten days that summer at the first Prospect Summer Institute. I came away with an exhilarating sense of having encountered a coherent theory with implications for practice not, to my knowledge, being articulated by any other educator in our time. (Brenda S. Engel, personal communication to a funding agency, February 1988)

During the seventies, the Prospect School evolved into a three-part institution: the school, the Prospect Institute for the Study of Meaning, and the Prospect Archive of Children's Work. (Its current designation is The Prospect Archive and Center for Education and Research.) The association with the NDSG remained strong: Members of the group made visits to the school, attended summer sessions for education and research, and used the resources of children's work in it's archives. In fact, the Prospect Center became something like an associated network, its list of participants overlapping that of the NDSG.

The group of teachers from Philadelphia, mentioned earlier in this chapter as having felt at times like "token" practitioners at NDSG meetings, have been closely involved with the Prospect Center over the years. Designating themselves the Philadelphia Teachers' Learning Cooperative (PTLC for short), this voluntary group has had a remarkable record of longevity—twenty-six years. The group, mostly made up of practicing public school teachers, holds weekly open meetings in participants' homes for the purpose of discussing and supporting worthwhile school practices.

> At the core of our meetings is a particular kind of conversation guided by the descriptive format developed by Patricia Carini and colleagues at the Prospect Center. These formats include procedures for describing a single child; a child's work such as writing, drawing, explanations of mathematical ideas; the work of a class such as whole-group discussions. In addition, we discuss our own work and larger educational issues. In anything we do, we try to focus on the strengths of children and teachers. **Most of our meetings end with implications for the classroom. (Statement distributed informally by the PTLC)**

The teachers in the Philadelphia TLC have been outspoken advocates of progressive school practices in their work, writings, and political activities. Carini herself, although not a political activist in the sense of joining picket lines or testifying before state legislatures, is essentially political in her outlook and dedication to the aims of equity and access held by Lillian Weber and other members of the NDSG. Her ability to accept and appreciate all children without the usual assumptions about "educability" because of background or ethnicity gave her a strong affinity with the NDSG's political stance and struggles. Patricia Carini and Lillian Weber were dramatically different in style, background, and kind of educational setting in which they worked but the close friendship that developed between them was based, in part, on commonly held beliefs in educational progressivism; equal access to good schooling; and, above all, the well-being of children.

> I was at that first meeting called by Vito in Grand Forks in 1972 to talk about evaluation, and more specifically, to challenge mandatory standardized testing and to seek ways to influence evaluation of children's growth and learning. Much about that meeting remains vivid in memory. This isn't the time for those memories. What I do want to select from that first meeting is that it was a gathering—a gathering of experiences and points of view on a matter, as Lillian says, of first importance: How to make room in schools for children to grow and learn, how to make schools that are rich resources for that growth, how to have the flourishing of the child be the standard for what is "good education," how to have an evaluation that starts from these first commitments. (Carini 1994, 14)

In addition to the educators whose work is mentioned in the preceding pages, others present in Grand Forks in 1972 were directors of progressive Follow Through sponsors, students of Perrone, or members of his staff. All brought to the table their own experiences and frustrations with traditional methods of evaluation. The tone of the conversation set by that original group and the implicitly and explicitly held values that informed those conversations has shaped the NDSG for over three decades.

As others joined later, they broadened the compass of concerns and enriched the group's thinking and intellectual experience. The membership became more diverse in several ways—race, culture, experience, work, age, and geographic location. The original themes to do with evaluation branched and twigged over the years although regularly returning to the root issue—evaluation itself. Those who came consistently to annual meetings were attracted by a shared vision of possibility, even when (which was most of the time) the vision seemed somewhere "off in left field"—certainly a minority view.

Those joining more recently have brought their own areas of knowledge, personalities, and passions to the group. It would be reductive to try to summarize here the variety, depth, and significance of their interests and contributions, although many of these will be represented in the chapters that constitute the body of this book. Participants can be characterized as generally steadfast in their commitment to a set of commonly held values with regard to schooling and the politics of democracy.

For many of us directly involved, the NDSG has been at the center of our professional lives. It has provided comfort and intellectual companionship to individuals in their allegiance to unpopular tenets and a sense of worth derived from being afloat in the same boat with thoughtful, respected, engaged, and remarkable colleagues. The Study Group has also had an important function on the wider scene by "holding values"—helping to keep them, to some extent, within the national consciousness. The values stem from the conjunction of two visions: the political one of true participatory democracy, and the related educational one of child-centered, progressive practice. Both are inclusive—for everyone.

III: The Progressive Tradition

Adherence to a general set of beliefs has kept the North Dakota Study Group together and ongoing for more than thirty years—beliefs about what constitutes worthwhile, relevant education for a democratic society. Like most beliefs, however, they were not born yesterday. The pedigree of progressive education can be traced back at least as far as the mid-seventeenth century. Between then and now, thinkers and practitioners, although living in radically different societies and under very different circumstances, came up with ideas that have strong implications for the present and that are still being argued over, played out, credited, and discredited.

There are two strands to the story: First, the relatively recent recognition that childhood is a distinct phase of life, not simply preparation for adulthood but worthy of respect and study in its own right; Second, the change in view of what is proper subject matter for education—a breaking away from the strict confines of the academy and becoming engaged with the surrounding physical, social, and moral world.

I will refer briefly to the work of a few of the thinkers who are the most interesting and seem to be significant to the history of the NDSG, to set the stage for the chapters that follow.

In the 1600s, John Amos Comenius was one of the first to record on paper some of the values still current among progressive educators. In his emphasis on learning as developmental, progressing from concrete experience to abstract thought, Comenius anticipated some of Piaget's discoveries by several centuries. His guiding image for appropriate curriculum was the natural growth of the tree, its form becoming increasingly complex as the trunk divides into branches, the branches into twigs.

Comenius also expressed remarkably modern, democratic views on access to education, recommending the use of the vernacular instead of texts available only in Greek and Latin and seeing education as a *universal entitlement* (to inject a contemporary term): "Not the children of the rich or of the powerful only but of all alike, boys and girls, noble and ignoble, rich and poor, in all cities and towns, villages and hamlets, should be sent to school" (1896/1657, 218).

In the following century, Jean-Jacques Rousseau was also concerned with issues of equality, railing in his writings against social and political injustices. In *The Social Contract* (1756), Rousseau laid down his precepts for a democratic society, opening with the poignant and ever-resonant statement: "Man is born free and everywhere he is in chains." In his best-known work on education, *Emile* (1762), Rousseau, like Comenius, turns for guidance to natural forms of development and growth. He contrasts the benign influence of nature to the pernicious one of corrupt man-made institutions, society in particular being deemed unnatural.

The child, Emile, was to learn from direct observation of nature and through experience with concrete objects in his immediate environment. He would thus build not only knowledge and understanding but would develop enough inner strength to enable him, later on, to resist the temptations and corruptions of society. Rousseau saw human intelligence as a development from the earliest stage of feelings, through those of the senses and intellect to the final stage of conscience or soul. Eventually Emile would emerge from the woods and join society, but as a strong, wholesome, resistant man.

Although evaluation as such was not then an issue, both Comenius and Rousseau emphasized the logic and efficacy of intrinsic motivation for encouraging learners—interest in the world and its workings—as opposed to negative motivation through punishment. In the late eighteenth century, Pestalozzi, a Swiss school master, put the theories of Comenius and Rousseau into practice, adding his own interpretations.

Pestalozzi's ideal curriculum was based on the use and observation of ordinary objects in the home and the activities of everyday domestic life. All children, no matter what their social station, were children of God and deserved the power-giving benefits of education. He recommended manual work to cultivate students' attention span, memory, and powers of observation. Although primarily a practitioner, Pestalozzi wrote several books on education that have had a wide influence in Europe and America (1781,

1801). His emphasis on immediate experience and observation as sources of understanding put Pestalozzi in the same general tradition as Comenius and Rousseau. (Pestalozzi's strict pedagogical methodologies—for instance, prescribed steps in reading instruction—now seem rigid, however, more like *Hooked on Phonics* than *Whole Language*.)

Friedrich Froebel, the inventor of the kindergarten ("children's garden") in the nineteenth century, also starts his educational agenda with the senses and immediate perception. He echoes his antiestablishment, romantic precursors in seeing nature as the ultimate teacher, cautioning schoolteachers against trying to interfere with the natural growth of children.

> We grant space and time to young plants and animals because we know that, in accordance with the laws that live in them, they will develop properly and grow well; young animals and plants are given rest, and arbitrary interference with their growth is avoided, because it is known that the opposite practice would disturb their pure unfolding and sound development; but the young human being is looked upon as a piece of wax, a lump of clay, which man can mold into what he pleases. (Froebel 1900, 8)

One of the most important enduring, longtime benefits of Froebel's pedagogy is the strong case he made for the educational and human value of play. "Play is the highest phase of child development—of human development at this period" and "the germinal leaves of all later life" (1900, 55). Beginning at home, then further cultivated in the "children's garden," play is at the center of the child's "natural life."

For Comenius, Rousseau, Pestalozzi, and Froebel, God and Nature are almost indistinguishable. The good life—the moral, spiritual life—is the natural life; although how that was interpreted depended of course on the place and the period as well as on the personal experience of the writer. The natural life implies an organic curriculum, one adapted to the child's broadening awareness and capabilities.

What struck me while reviewing the work of these four theorists of education is their persistent, focused, and central concern with the child, his or (occasionally) her welfare, happiness, and growth. Their recommended practices would now be called *child-centered*. Traces of Froebel's influence and, from further back, the writings of Comenius, Rousseau, and Pestalozzi can be seen in the 1967 document known as The Plowden Report issued by an official British government commission on education:

> At the heart of the educational process lies the child. No advances in policy, no acquisitions of new equipment have their desired effect unless they are in harmony with the nature of the child, unless they are fundamentally acceptable to him. (73)

This document provided the rationale for the integrated day in the early grades, in England, and, indirectly, for open education in the United States.

The most immediate influence on progressive education, John Dewey, lived (and wrote for much of) a phenomenal ninety-three years, from 1859 to 1952. Relatively early in his life, when still in his thirties, he opened an experimental school in Chicago as a laboratory for his theories about education. (It later became, and in fact still is, the Laboratory School of the University of Chicago.) During this time, Dewey published "My Pedagogic Creed," which laid out, in brief form, his then current thinking about schooling.

> This education process has two sides—one psychological and one sociological and neither can be subordinated to the other, or neglected, without evil results following. Of these two sides, the psychological is the basis. The child's own instincts and powers furnish the materials and give the starting point for all education. (1897, 77)

Education of the "psychological side" begins at home and develops in accordance with the child's nature—his "powers, interests, and habits." The school, as community, then represents "present life"—life as real and vital to the child as that which he carries on in the home, in the neighborhood, or on the playground." Although Rousseau, in *Emile,* exalts nature in dramatic contrast to society and is bitterly critical of the latter, Dewey sees education itself as inseparable from social (or community) knowledge. In a later work, he takes this issue on directly:

> The seeming antisocial philosophy [of the eighteenth century] was a somewhat transparent mask for an impetus toward a wider and freer society—toward cosmopolitanism. . . . The emancipated individual was to become the organ and agent of a comprehensive and progressive society. (Dewey 1944, 91–2)

Dewey's attempt to reconcile his theories of progressivism with those of his predecessors, particularly Rousseau, came from an apparent wish to integrate them into the thinking and practices of his own times, the industrial age. Dewey, like them, writes about the child's nature being the touchstone for instruction but gives equal urgency to the cause of educating for a progressive society. Like them also and along with his belief in science, Dewey affirms a belief in God. "My Pedagogic Creed" ends with a description of the teacher as "the prophet of the true God and the usherer in of the true kingdom of God" (1897, 80).

Dewey's Chicago Lab School virtually defined progressive education. It was created specifically to test his theories of education (and, almost equally important to Dewey, to provide good schooling for his own children). On November 1, 1894, he wrote this to his wife, Alice:

> I sometimes think I will drop teaching phil [sic]—directly & teach it via pedagogy. When you think of the thousands & thousands of young'uns who are practically being ruined negatively if not positively in the Chicago schools every year, it is enough to make you go out & howl on the street corners like the Salvation Army. There is an image of a school growing up in my mind all the time; a school where some actual & literal constructive activity shall be the centre & source of the whole thing, & from which the work should be always growing out in two directions—one the social bearings of that constructive industry, the other the contact with nature which supplies it with its materials. (Menand 2001, 319)

Louis Menand, in *The Metaphysical Club*, further explains Dewey's view:

> By "unity of knowledge" Dewey did not mean that all knowledge is one. He meant that knowledge is inseparably united with doing. Education at the Dewey School was based on the idea that knowledge is a by-product of activity: people do things in the world, and the doing results in learning something that, if deemed useful, gets carried along into the next activity. In the traditional method of education, in which the things considered worth knowing are handed down from teacher to pupil as disembodied information, knowledge is cut off from the activity in which it has meaning and becomes a false abstraction. One of the consequences (besides boredom) is that an invidious distinction between knowing and doing—a distinction Dewey thought socially pernicious as well as philosophically erroneous—gets reinforced. (2001, 322)

This idea, the inseparability of "knowing and doing" is, I believe, at the heart of the matter. In the penultimate sentence of Part II of this introduction, I wrote, "The values [of the NDSG] stem from the conjunction of two visions: the political one of true participatory democracy, and the related educational one of child-centered, progressive practice." All the theories, experiences, and practices described by the authors in this book can be accommodated within this conjunction—or, in Dewey's words, "experiential continuum" (1963, 33).

The educational enterprise itself can be seen as having two facets, one more inner—home-based, reflective, and in harmony with the nature of the child; the other more outward—in-the-world, communal, moral, and political. Both, constantly interactive, are essential to a progressive education. Learning starts at home, in the child's immediate surround, and as the child enters school, she moves out, though not away from her beginnings. The image is more one of an expanding circle than a road being traveled. When she enters school, she comes already equipped with her early interests, habits, knowledge, skills, feelings, and character (e.g., curiosity, playfulness, inwardness or outwardness, sense of humor).

Children (or adults) learn different things in different ways, some of them more "inner" some more "outer." They learn through activities and experiences, observation and reflection, participation, imitation, social communication. These means of gaining knowledge and understanding blend together; at times, one (or a combination of several) dominates depending on the particular nature of what is being learned.

An example: My grandson, Will, has accumulated in his twelve years of life what seems to me an impressive knowledge of baseball. By a rough estimate I would say that Will is familiar with the facts about many (most?) of the players on most of the major league teams—their statistics, styles, professional and sometimes personal histories. He also knows a lot about the teams and their competitive records going back fifty or sixty years. He has a thorough grasp of the rules of the game and understands the subtleties of signals, strategies, and decision making, as well as the authority that goes with the various roles and positions in the baseball hierarchy. Complex stuff. And Will is by no means exceptional in his control over this extensive body of knowledge. They all seem to know it, Will and his friends.

So the question is, how did it happen? The answer: In all the ways I just listed, seamlessly blended. Will shares his intense interest in the game with his father (my son) who was equally involved as a child and continues to enjoy baseball now as a spectator sport. Will goes to baseball games and often watches games on television. He plays on a Little League team and does hours of batting and throwing practice at home with his father. Will and his friends talk endlessly about their favorite players and teams. They collect and trade baseball cards, analyze and find meaning in baseball statistics, read the sports section in the newspaper, read and discuss baseball novels. They have become experts—with no instruction. No one explained to Will why a runner has to touch first base before going on to second, the fact that there are three "bases" and one "plate" or what constitutes an "error." In current jargon, this is called *holistic learning*. One might equally well call it "contextualized learning" or, when teacher-guided, even "progressive education."

In considering the two facets of education, the personal and the political, the most urgent these days in both are questions of equity and access which include, of course, issues around racism. In John Dewey's day, concern with social justice had a somewhat different focus—more on poverty and the status of immigrants, problems that are still urgent and unsolved. But in recent years the dramatic growth of minority populations, the legal empowerment of African Americans during the Civil Rights Movement—the rising voice of the disenfranchised and underprivileged of all ethnicities—has changed the moral and political landscape and radically altered the terms of the discussion. Any words or actions of progressive educators must deal first with issues of diversity, access, and equity and with those who have traditionally been denied, or short-changed, on all three.

The chapters that follow are bound together by their authors' general subscription to the values of progressivism. They have been somewhat arbitrarily grouped under six headings—"arbitrarily" because the same concerns tend to pop up throughout, ideas echo back and forth along with the names of certain hovering tutelary spirits cited by many authorial voices (John Dewey most often!).

Notes

1. Part II of this introduction goes more deeply into the beliefs and values held in common by these educators who eventually called themselves the North Dakota Study Group on Evaluation.

2. The group included Patricia Carini, cofounder and researcher at the Prospect School—a small, independent school in Vermont; director George Hein and Margaret DiRiviera from Follow Through at the Education Development Center in Newton, Massachusetts; Shirley Childs from the University of Connecticut Follow Through directed by Vincent Rogers; Edward A. Chittenden and Anne M. Bussis, research psychologists in the early childhood unit at Educational Testing Service, Princeton, New Jersey; Lillian Weber, professor of Early Childhood Education at City College in New York and director of Advisory Services to the Open Corridors Program in the city public schools; Deborah Meier, an advisor in Weber's program as well as coordinator of Open Education in District 2, New York City; Ann Cook and Herb Mack, codirectors of the Community Resources Institute, which also offered advisory services to the New York City public schools; Elizabeth Gilkerson, director of the Bank Street College Follow Through; Bob Gaines of the Follow Through program at Fort Yates sponsored by UND; Chuck Nielsen, Linda Harness, and Nancy Miller from the Center for Teaching and Learning, UND; Joe Grannis, professor at Teachers College, Columbia; and Michael Patton, doctoral candidate at the University of Wisconsin and consultant to the UND Follow Through.

PART ONE

Progressive Education

This first section includes chapters that clarify the traditional beliefs, values, and practices of progressive education. Vito Perrone, the original convener of the North Dakota Study Group and for many years its central figure, gave a summary of the progressive agenda in a talk to the group in February 2000. It appears here in the form of an article that lays out our commonly agreed-on formulations and goes on to identify the major obstacles to their achievement.

Next, Beth Alberty and Ruth Dropkin introduce an article by Lillian Weber, a much revered and influential educator and powerful, articulate figure at the NDSG meetings. In this chapter Weber, who died in 1994, identifies the broad sources of progressivism in the worlds of politics, social work, literature, and early childhood education as well as personal sources in her own history.

Joseph Featherstone outlines some of the challenges, the "big themes," that educators inevitably face today and with which we must contend in order to move forward into a world more consistent with our values. Alice Seletsky reminds us of the many wonderful books of the sixties, which we all read and which changed our thinking along with our teaching. Finally, Edie Klausner gives a lyrical though real-life account of what a good school can mean, for both adults and children.

1

The Progressive Agenda

VITO PERRONE

As members of the North Dakota Study Group we come from many different places and approach education from diverse vantage points—classrooms and schools, colleges and universities, research and policy institutes, and advocacy and community organizing enterprises. Nonetheless we share important social commitments and particular visions of what is possible in schools and communities. While we might not subscribe equally to the whole of the long-standing progressive agenda, we tend to agree on at least some of the following formulations:

- Children and young people possess unlimited potential for making personal meanings of the world; powerful learning is in their grasp.
- Creative energies are universal though too often unacknowledged and supported.
- Responsibility, a sense of personal and community empowerment, can be cultivated.
- Teachers can be curriculum builders, decision makers, serious students of teaching.
- Education can be conceived as expansive, as intensely personal and simultaneously cooperative, as living and interpretive, and imaginative.
- Constructive pluralism and democracy are both possible, worth struggling for.
- The longtime promise of equality along with personal and community well-being should, and can, be translated into reality.

Source: Adapted by the editor from an address to the NDSG, in February 2000.

I have felt it important from time to time to reaffirm some of the pieces of the fabric that has bound us over these many years, to suggest again that regardless of the circumstances that surround us, no matter how difficult or discouraging it might seem, those large understandings need to be held, the cracks found, possibilities kept alive. Accommodation, Martin Luther King reminded us, is always the easier path but "it won't lead to the promised land" (King 1968). And we want that promised land of social justice for children and young people, for the schools, for the larger society.

Our joining together in 1972 came at a time not too dissimilar from the present. Recalling the context, though, may be useful. For almost a decade prior to that first meeting, we had been living with a socially and educationally progressive renaissance. The civil rights struggles were often bitter but it seemed that the shackles were breaking, that a new America, a more racially democratic America, was in view. It was a time of educational hopefulness—around new schools, integrated learning, greater inclusiveness. Students were engaged in long-term projects—actually doing something in depth based on their own interests and intentions—in classrooms and schools where genuine performance mattered. Active learning was being reinvented. There was discourse about learning making connections to students' lives beyond school and the importance of schools and communities becoming more integrated. Teachers were being spoken of as scholars, intellectuals, readers, and writers who saw their work as contributing to making their communities better, providing their students and families a larger view of possibilities. There was support for pluralism, for equity, for democracy. Caring and respect were formulations with meaning, and efforts were being made to put them into practice.

Although I realize that I am putting forward with insufficient complexity a characterization of a period of time that has been described by social conservatives as filled with moral decay and the destruction of the schools, I think it is important to remind us of that time as progressive and constructive, even as I don't want to imply that the flowering was universal. The struggles were huge and schools remained for the most part as they had long been, mostly conserving institutions. Nonetheless, it was a period when genuine experimentation was possible, given reasonable encouragement, and the discourse was mostly hopeful. It was for many of us with progressive–democratic visions, the biggest crack in the social–educational–economic armor we had ever seen.

By 1972, however, a rapidly growing backlash against sixties values was gaining enormous strength—against much of the language of freedom and in opposition to the democratic localism that supported so much variation of practices. It should have been anticipated, given the unraveling situation in Vietnam and an economy beginning to stall and the social debates about values growing. But we were not very well prepared.

State testing, commonplace in America's schools at the close of the nineteenth century and again in the twenties and thirties, returned, this time, however, with a fury of charges that the schools were failing. The talk was of *accountability*, a new word in the educational lexicon, defined as determining what the public was getting for its expenditures on public education. Test scores, now being published for the first time in the newspapers, began to matter more than projects or the arts or public service or locally invented curriculum.

Test preparation materials were being offered to improve the scores. This, too, was new. By 1977, competency tests were in place in thirty-six states, with the need to meet some related score for promotion and graduation firmly in place. That the burden of failure fell disproportionately on the most disenfranchised populations—on African Americans, Latinos, the poor—was not deemed by policy makers as reason to alter the practice. It was just a matter of accountability, of supporting old-time merit, the essence of America's promise. It was, as I was told at the time, a short-term sacrifice that some students and schools would have to live through. In a decade, supporters noted most students will pass the tests because those in schools will work harder.

I won't play out the story, the trail to *A Nation at Risk* (1983), to even more tests, to interest in greater standardization. How could such a document with so little social–cultural–education evidence have played so well in the media? In those complicated, backlash years, members of the Study Group challenged the directions, continued to write about more powerful possibilities for the schools, found allies in parents, and convinced many state legislators that some space needed to be provided for a different vision of education. While we didn't cause any large sea change, we were influential in getting the open-testing law passed in New York State, which made the SAT and other such tests open to review, and our persistence dented some of the standardizing momentum.

Surprisingly, given the political climate, a new window of progressive opportunity opened in the last half of the eighties, part of what some of the governors called the second wave of reform. They suggested the first wave, with all the heavy testing and standardization, was necessary to get everyone's attention and now some choices could be made to support the schools that had learned how to be better. It was patronizing, but it provided a larger crack than had been seen for at least a decade. During this period, members of the NDSG helped organize new schools and generated, by their language and practices, new hopes for another progressive renaissance. States began to back away from graduation tests and the heavy prescription of curriculum. Many schools sought and were granted waivers from various state regulations. Schools supported inclusion and performance, using the language of reinvention, individualization, and democracy again. They embraced parents and communities. The idea of commonwealth—that schools could provide something personal and lasting—was resurrected. Even John Dewey and W. E. B. DuBois were dusted off the shelves, read again, seen as inspiring. It was, though, all short-lived and in a number of ways we went back again to our beginnings as a Study Group.

The language of standards—though increasingly coming to mean standardization—fills the media. It is the talk of legislators, of governors, of the president and presidential candidates, of those who lead the largest of our corporations. The tests, for purposes of promotion and graduation, have returned with a vengeance that could hardly have been anticipated, and they are rooted in a more common curriculum than could have been imagined. We are being told that we now know what every student should know and be able to do, grade level by grade level, and it now makes sense to have a common curriculum. Habits of mind don't make the lists. Waivers are out, viewed as anachronisms of another time when the knowledge everyone needed was less clear.

The absurdity of current conditions is so great that it is difficult to discuss it seriously. Who could imagine making single tests stand for everything, rendering meaningless most of what teachers and students do day in and day out, on the premise that holding everyone's feet to the proverbial fire will bring about the highest levels of achievement that can be imagined. There is nothing in our history that would support such a claim.

In many settings test prep is becoming the curriculum. Failure rates on various high-stakes tests are extraordinarily high and match perfectly, as such tests have for as long as they have been given, race and socioeconomic factors. Some state officials expressed surprise that students in the wealthiest communities did better than students in less well-to-do and poor communities. This is another level of the absurdity.

The high failure rates across the country—though not corroborated by many other standardized test measures from the Stanford 9 to the SAT—are unfortunately helping build the case for more voucher experiments, more charter schools, more privatization. Support for public schooling seems to erode with each report on state testing. I don't see any evidence that schools are getting better through this testing and standards mania. But there is considerable evidence of increasing dropout rates, especially among African American, Latinos, limited English speakers, special needs students, and students from economically poor families. This doesn't bode well for our democratic hopes.

There is, however, a growing response. Across the country, in many cases led by parents and students in growing alliance with teachers, the arguments are getting better, rooted in a call for higher-quality education and the more genuine accountability that can come only from local initiative and commitment. The argument that using a single test to determine everything, which is indefensible educationally and morally, is beginning to resonate.

Unlike the earlier time, when the Study Group was just forming, however, there are large numbers of schools in place—many more than in 1972—that remain steadfast in their uniqueness, in their progressive and democratic directions. The Small Schools movement, which began in the mid-eighties, led initially by the pioneering work of Deborah Meier and Ann Cook in New York, Bill Ayers in Chicago, Linda Nathan and Larry Myatt in Boston, Ana Maria Garcia Blanco in Puerto Rico, and Ted Sizer through the Coalition, among others, has flowered. Numbering in the thousands, these schools have generated large-scale support through their emphasis on active learning and exhibitions and graduation by performance. They have become the standard-bearers of the good education that almost everyone wants. While under pressure in the current political climate, they are not letting go of their larger visions. The odds seem better than they appeared in the mid-seventies, for example. That is the positive news. But we have to enlarge our vistas.

While I am optimistic about many aspects of our work, I worry about our long-term struggle for a more integrated, fully democratic society. Support for affirmative action and desegregation has virtually collapsed in the face of recent court rulings, public ballot initiatives, and a generally timid response from educators and their allies. And a meanness of spirit in regard to matters of race and class has grown.

What are we doing to support a different view, a more democratic view? Dewey wrote of the need to bring "intelligent sympathy" (1944, 121) to our work as educators, that need to feel the social situations of others, to pay attention to the objective conditions of others, to walk with others. How do we engage matters of race and class in our schools? What kinds of experiences are we providing for our students? Are we arguing as effectively as we can the case for democratic schools and a democratic society? This must be our ongoing commitment. Anything less is more of the accommodation that we see growing around us. We need to again heed the words of Martin Luther King (1963): The reason we haven't succeeded fully with the civil rights struggle is because of "the appalling silence of the good people." We need to help break the silence everywhere. We need to continue to see our work as always larger than schools. That was Dewey's message. It was DuBois' message. It must be our ongoing imperative.

2

The Roots of Open Education

LILLIAN WEBER
INTRODUCTION BY BETH ALBERTY AND RUTH DROPKIN

Introduction

Lillian Weber wrote the following as the introduction for the proceedings of a 1975 conference, which was published by the Workshop Center for Open Education at City College, New York, under the title *Roots of Open Education in America: Reminiscences and Reflections* (1976). That paperback contains transcripts of talks and photographs on themes ranging from Native American life to WPA programs to Yiddish *shules,* as well as theoretical pieces on science and early childhood curriculums and a history of school reform in the United States by Vito Perrone.

The conference in itself was a singular—one might even say, historic—event, bringing together as it did participants in the Civil Rights Movement such as Myles Horton and Dorothy Cotton; pioneers of early childhood education such as Charlotte Winsor and Caroline Pratt; leaders in social work such as Helen Hall and H. Daniel Carpenter; important thinkers in education such as David Hawkins and Vito Perrone; veteran teachers of the public and private schools and of after-school programs such as Walter Clark, Vincent Wright, Louis Cohen, Mary Burks, Neva Laroque Howrigan, and Claudia Lewis; authorities on Black Studies such as Osborne E. Scott; and popular analysts such as Joseph Featherstone and Paul Nash. This participation, rich as it was in reviving old connections between people and programs and making new ones, resulted from staff proposing one name that led to another, but conference planners acknowledged that limited resources of time, staff, and money meant that they hardly touched the Western experience and not at all, to their regret, the Hispanic.

All the contributors represented significant sources of value to the changes in the public schools Lillian Weber and her cohorts were working to bring about. And so, as leader in the effort referred to as open education, Weber organized and led the one-day meeting held at the City College of New York.

At the outset, Weber asks, "Why a conference on the Roots of Open Education in the spring of 1975?" Her answer—the ever-present need to reconnect with the past so that new developments can be understood and reflected on as solid, substantial commitments—is the larger part of the story. Unmentioned, but also important, was the then unfolding threat to those new developments from the New York City school system as it responded to the city's budget crisis of the mid-1970s. As teachers were fired, and others reassigned on the basis of seniority, the new learning communities Weber and her colleagues had helped teachers, parents, and principals build in the schools were abruptly dismantled. Teachers accustomed to working collaboratively and to having some authority over their classroom schedule, organization, and curriculum were uprooted and found themselves in teaching environments less amenable to their ideas. They might be determined to maintain their commitments to active learning responsive to children's individual interests and pace of growth, but their morale was battered. Weber, always ingenious in finding ways to support teachers in their progressive work, offered them, in *Roots*, a connection with an affirmative history—much of it oral, embodied in living individuals from older and various traditions, from out-of-school as well as in-school venues—of the broad and varied nature of striving for education that is based on valuing the intelligence and originality of every human being.

In the current education climate of standardization and attack on the individual nature and value of each child, this is still a message from which to draw strength.

Introduction to the Conference Proceedings, December 1976

Why a conference on the Roots of Open Education in the spring of 1975 and why one that had the particular shape of this one? What did we, working in a framework collectively identified, for better or worse, as *open education*, hope to clarify beyond what was already obvious to many of us—namely, that so much of the discussion about open education to that point seemed to fall within the absurd context of "new developments" without a history or a past? What beyond the fact that many of us saw a clear need for a revival of the past as a living force to be interpreted and reinterpreted? We knew that we needed to reconnect to our past, but which past? And for what meanings of open education?

From what past had I drawn my own commitments? Were they indeed derived, as I had reported, from my study of institutional examples and theoretical formulations of progressive education, my study at the Bank Street College of Education, my work as a nursery school teacher? Certainly these were resources on which I drew. In fact, with so little in contemporary psychological research showing any awareness of the continuities in children's development, as well as of the function of time, I had found it necessary to reexamine the serious longitudinal child development studies from Iowa, Merrill-Palmer, Bank Street, and the Dewey School experience.

What I recognized in these studies of informal education and in ideas generally embodied by informal education, was the context of life as it existed for me in my childhood. It existed for me in my memories of kitchen smells—of baked apples and rice pudding—of all of us working at our different things at the round oak table, under the hanging lamp. Where and when did I begin to feel for the natural world? My memories—always with my father or an older brother or sister—are of dew, of early morning mists, of first swimming, of the harvest moon, blood red and hanging low. It was with all these memories that I resonated to the truth of the description of prior-to-school learning. If I had not recognized the roots in life itself, my Bank Street studies would have remained disembodied theory.

As I talked with parents about open education, they all, to greater or lesser degree, expressed these recognitions too: the bypassing incidental focus, the intimacies, the awareness—in all families of more than one child—of difference, of sense of place and acceptance, of being included, of continuity in relatedness. All of this they saw as the stuff of the prior-to-school context.

For myself as middle child in a big family, perhaps more had existed than such generalized and universal aspects of prior-to-school learning. I remember that there was *room* for me to be reflective about my place in the family. I was allowed to present a "stone face" to the enormously rich life around me, *while* I made an effort to understand it. Our household was based on respect for the person; the constant self-assessment and examination of ideas and of personality and character differences in the household was a conscious teaching environment.

There was a very strong assumption in my family, perhaps because of its size, of diversity and difference among all of us. Certainly, one had to get along in this family, but the idea of adjusting to some standard did not exist in quite the way it is discussed today. In my family, strong support for and loyalty to each other and to the family were taken for granted, but apparently differences could exist within this extremely strong social framework.

I remembered other experiences, all voluntary, all external to school structures—each of us choosing from the array of offerings during the two weeks of Chautauqua, when I lived in West Virginia, and then the discussions that followed for many more weeks. I remember my father's comment on labor schools; his own education through union work; the experiences I heard described, when I lived in Virginia, of those who worked with the Highlander Folk School; discussions about how to fight the poll tax and about rural electrification.

There was even more in the surroundings of my growing up years than the intimacies I later recognized when reading the descriptions that bolstered discussions of developmental theory. There were the recognitions of my immigrant family culture in the books I read. The literary societies described in *The Little House on the Prairie* (Wilder 1935) had their parallel in the Jewish P. E. N. clubs, which welcomed recitals of my mother's poetry. My mother, who was a child of her culture, spoke to us about the dancer Isadora Duncan and the cause of freedom and expression for the human body. She would illustrate a point with the work of those writers who were important to her—Tolstoy, Heine, Hugo. Although she was not at all interested in politics, she knew what was going on; the struggles and strivings of this or that group were alive in my household.

Understanding was a big word in my family. I was strongly conscious at all times of *trying* to understand, of striving to make sense. Education equated with understanding went on at all times—at the table, during walks, in all aspects of life. But I'm sure this consciousness about education was not a characteristic of my family alone. It was probably strong in all those of my parents' generation who were seeking to better things, who had to set up their own newspapers, their own voluntary societies, their own institutions to accomplish this. My father and his generation in the late nineteenth century were steeped in a rationalism and in a belief in progress and democracy that was based on the assertion of human potential, of human understanding. In my home, it was assumed that people were intelligent, that they were strong and capable, and that all were entitled to the dignity of humans.

Thus the continuities within the ideas of progressive education and the cultural context of my growing up are obvious. How could I not, drawing on such recollections, find obvious resonances in the later discussions on language acquisition, comprehension, IQ; the assumption of intelligence is central to my system of values. During the years I studied informal education in England, I was not surprised to discover that Robert Owen, a socialist, reacted to the horrors of the Industrial Revolution with a search for ways that would support the development of the potential in all children, for ways that could include all children in the enjoyment of their own childhood. I was not surprised that Susan Isaacs and the McMillan sisters, who picketed Parliament in 1917 for free nursery schools, also sought ways of making the world better: a standard of inclusiveness that embraced the right of all children to express their potentiality. That the kindergartens of Caroline Pratt and of the Ethical Culture Societies served the children of working-class families, and that they were organized for the purpose of being inclusive rather than exclusive, struck me as entirely natural.

What was it about these early experiences that related them to my later study? What indeed was central to these experiences and the development of open education? The community? The preservation of the cultural inheritance? The intergenerational character of the experiences? All these, and more, for inherent in all was an offering of educative experience to the learner without sorting mechanisms or certification systems or prior qualifications. Indeed, as I mulled over the experiences I had culled from my memories, it struck me how such offerings and such a welcome to the willing learner seemed to be the expectation of many groups in their vision of America; this was true particularly for the immigrants who, in their coming, challenged the deference to class and educational status and asserted themselves as people with potential. They organized cultural experiences to sustain themselves in this strange land; they joined educational enterprises—literary societies, singing clubs, and so on—to help map their own path to self-fulfillment, without Old-World constraints. They, of course, used the public schools, as well as these extra-school experiences, but it is clear from the number of communal educational groups that the schools provided insufficient nutrients for the ordinary person's drive for further development and cultural continuity.

It was confidence in the human as learner that inspired progressive educators; it was the natural ways in which human learning developed that they studied in their effort to revitalize the schools. Whatever their nationality—Froebel, Pestalozzi, Montessori—they drew on what they knew of the learner as observed in informal settings: family experiences and the communal cultural experiences, and they tried to figure out how to plan for, maintain, and keep continuous the vigor of this informal learning *within* the schools. The sensitive educators who planned the Dewey School, for instance, observing that for the American child of the late nineteenth and early twentieth centuries the informal educative experiences in the preindustrial frontier household were less available, attempted to revive their nutritive force in the learning process by including them in schools.

The ideas of open education, after all, are about the person; about difference; about continuity; about human striving to make both sense of the world and an impact on it; about potentiality and the conditions of life that nurture or suppress the flowering of potentiality; about the conditions that allow the recognition and emergence of ideas; and about the professional, theoretical, and institutional context of schooling. What is inherent to open education understood in this way is a broad acceptance of all humans as part of the group and value and respect for all persons as active learners, capable of intelligent, active efforts to survive. It followed naturally for us to value stories of human experience—even more, stories of immigrant survival and the self-assertions of the oppressed. In these informal, historical accounts—whether novelistic or autobiographical accounts of how each group or each family unit, struggling to survive, organized cultural and personal experiences to sustain and fulfill a way of life—we found the roots of open education. And out of this understanding, which has blown life into our work at the Workshop Center for Open Education, we organized our conference. The all-day meeting, which drew an audience of more than 500 people, was a dramatic and often stirring convergence of old and young— those in the vanguard of today's efforts to restore humanistic values to schools as well as spokespersons for similar but older, even vanished, currents in American life.

Nor was this conference simply a nostalgia trip. Its evocation of the past was organized with the idea of confirming the continuity of those strands in our national life that encouraged self-development. By bringing together people whose experiences in informal organizations appeared to reinforce the truth about our contemporary belief in human educability, the conference hoped to reaffirm the humanistic wellspring of America. It created the opportunity for firsthand encounters with men and women who had played a vital part in programs predicated on faith in the educability of all people. Through informal, small-group interchanges, conference participants experienced the excitement of sharing in living history. Their sense of renewal flowed from the spirit and substance of the presentations they heard. What they were treated to was genuine oral history about persons, times, and ideas whose meaning, often overlooked, obscured, or bypassed, was this day given new life. Their appreciation was succinctly expressed by one participant: "When I thought back over the day, it struck me very forcibly: There is no culture without history. History gives feelings of connectedness. It refreshes you and lifts you."

3

Progressive, Democratic Education: A Primer

JOSEPH FEATHERSTONE

My grandmother was the teaching principal of a small, mostly immigrant elementary school in the Pennsylvania coal country—one of many Irish Catholics who took part in the progressive educational and political movements of her time. She was ambitious about kids' learning. The children of immigrant coal miners, whose fathers were often out of work, read high-class literature and poetry—she had a weakness for the English poet Robert Browning. She checked to see that kids brushed their teeth. My beloved Aunt Mary was a student in my grandmother's fourth-grade class. She remembered how strict it was. Like the others, Mary had her teeth checked. And Mary, too, had to not only memorize and recite a passage from Browning's poem, *Pippa Passes,* but also to explain its meaning in her own words.

My grandmother was a force in local and state politics, fighting for labor rights (her allies in politics were the United Mine Workers, whose leader was her hero, John Mitchell), pioneering in women's rights, and leading the movement to end child labor. She was the first woman elected to the state Democratic Committee. She saw a clear link between democratic politics and her teaching practice.

She was a domestic and classroom tyrant. Her teaching was almost certainly not what we think of as classic child-centered progressivism. There was, though, the interesting assumption that workers' kids should read the best literature—they should get whatever rich kids get. Asking for meaning, she invited a child to interpret and understand a poem, not just memorize it. The business about teeth says something too: She was concerned about the whole child, body as well as mind. The true basics in education were what kids would need to grow up healthy and well and to participate in the on-going creation of democracy.

I like to think that all this made my grandmother a variety of progressive teacher who is a constant in each generation of U.S. schooling, public as well as private. I believe they exist in growing numbers today: Teachers who don't necessarily wear a progressive or democratic label, but who have holistic, complex, democratic ambitions for all the kids they teach; teachers who aim at helping students of all backgrounds to partici-pate in politics and life and culture, not just pass a standardized test—to become actors and players, not just spectators.

In his beautiful primer on democracy, the "Gettysburg Address," Lincoln spoke of the United States as an experiment in government of, by, and for the people. The classroom counterpart would be an education of, by, and for the people. Lincoln, self-taught as he was, implied an ideal demo-cratic culture that has never existed, not even in the democracy of ancient Athens with its slaves and inferior status assigned to women. The great American progressive democrat John Dewey sums all this up (deliberately echoing Lincoln) in his classic, *Experience and Education* (1963/1938), by calling for an education "of, by, and for experience." Learning how to learn from experience—to act, to reflect on results, and then to take the next step thoughtfully—is Dewey's ideal of the educated person, an ideal that is never finished because experience keeps on going. Dewey was speaking in a long line of democratic thinkers and educators. Lincoln, Walt Whitman, W. E. B. DuBois, Margaret Haley, Leonard Covello, Myles Horton, Lucy Sprague Mitchell, Vito Perrone, and generations of less famous schoolteachers and parents have all dreamed of such an education and of such a culture for everybody's children. As with Lincoln's ideal of democratic politics, the es-sence would be the experience of active participation. Full participation in school now would be the best preparation for what DuBois called as the three goals of democratic education—the capacity to take part in "work, cul-ture, and liberty."

The founding members of the North Dakota Study Group thirty years ago came out of the revival of progressive education in the 1960s; they were also products of the Civil Rights Revolution. In the early 1970s they were re-sponding to the challenges—especially in areas such as testing and evalua-tion—of putting progressive educational and political values into place in public schools on a significant scale. They were trying to maintain the con-nection between classroom reform and egalitarian political reform. The thought and practice of the NDSG reflect the complex and many-sided goal of the creation of a better democracy in which students will grow up to be good citizens not only of their own nation, but also of the world. The group draws on, and adds to, a long record of more than a century of social, political, and educational practice that has opened up certain big themes as sites for investigation. The themes can be thought of as questions or problems that each generation of progressive teachers and parents have explored. My friend the late John Holt used to warn that "a conservative is someone who worships a dead radical." Each new generation needs to write its own fresh chapter. But the experience of the past is a help in rethinking the present. The following are some of the big themes I see when I look around at the work of my colleagues and friends.

1. Walt Whitman wrote: "It [democracy] is a great word whose history, I suppose, remains unwritten because that history has yet to be enacted" (1871/1949, 8). The progressive emphasis on schools as democratic communities is important and necessary in its own right as an ideal in opposition to many of the reigning market, corporate, and consumerist visions of education; it ought to figure more prominently in a nation and world facing unprecedented immigration, dislocation, and the movement of peoples around the planet. This is the time of greatest immigration in all of U.S. history. City, suburban, and even rural schools are encountering immigrant families. It seems truly bizarre to us progressives that therefore one of the major policy themes today is the drive to standardize and tighten bureaucratic control over teachers, teaching, and classrooms. The diverse population in schools today would be far better served if more educators felt free to adopt the stance toward immigrants and historic outsiders of Leonard Covello, the teaching principal of Benjamin Franklin High School in New York City during the 1930s (see Perrone's wonderful 1998 book, *Teacher with a Heart*). Covello argued for schools as democratic communities, welcoming families and capitalizing on diversity. He devoted much thought to ways of reaching out to families and personalizing learning for individual kids, helping schools become networks connecting families and communities, and taking advantage of the languages and experiences and knowledge immigrant families bring to America. He was a pioneer in teaching ethnic studies and in promoting understanding, tolerance, and coalition-building among the groups that make up the American rainbow. For Covello, running a school and teaching are forms of democratic community organizing.

2. Another challenge for schools and families today has to do with the ecology of childhood—the task of making schools and other settings good environments and communities in which children develop as whole and healthy people—not test factories where kids get evaluated in one-sided ways. The progressive–democratic tradition is built on a vision of childhood as a time of imagination, construction, and growth through understanding

and action—and schools as communities that link adults to children in relationships of care. The social, the intellectual, and the aesthetic are not separate in this complex tradition of teaching. In an era of school reform driven by managerial values and test scores, progressives remind us to keep focused on the quality of schools as places for the growth of children. Progressives share the worries of many families about child care, and the amount of time kids now spend outside of the family in impersonal formal institutions such as schools, day-care settings, after-school programs, and the like. School policies framed in the light of progressive values would, for example, emphasize aligning schools with families and childrearing, particularly in this time of enormous pressure on families of all social classes. Our current policies seem to be the work of men (I choose my word deliberately) who don't have a clue about childhood and families and their needs. The care of children from morning to evening is a concern that touches families across the spectrum of social classes. Most families need much better support for childrearing than they are getting. The opposite is what they are getting in fact—a corporate vision of education as a grading and testing machine to produce a workforce. The quality of children's lives and the relationships between kids and grownups ought to be central concerns of educational policy, yet they scarcely appear in all the stacks of current standards. Progressives demand a more personalized and communal vision of education—a social and emotional, as well as an academic apprenticeship to growing up. Childhood at present, like our forests and wetlands, is at risk from the developers and *Gradgrinds* who have highjacked policy.

3. The progressive tradition these days also offers a small but growing and important body of classroom work in all the school subjects that suggests possible pathways toward the relatively new (in U.S. and world history) democratic goal of educating all students for participation in intellectual and academic complexity. Americans continue to disagree as they always have about the elements of a decent education but most would agree that the demands of work, citizenship, culture, and perhaps even such aspects of life as parenting have grown more complex and demanding. Formal schooling and educational credentials play a greater role in people's lives. A fair expectation, for example, is that most students in school now will at some time enroll in some form of higher or further education. In any case, being good at school matters more than it used to. Being bad at school is especially disastrous if you are working class or dark-skinned or poor. Conservatives and progressives all have a stake in schools where most kids (not just an elite) know and understand more than in a simpler era. More

and more Americans now agree with my grandmother and Deborah Meier that poor kids deserve what the rich kids are getting—an intellectually ambitious education.

Despite the current talk about high standards and academic and intellectual complexity, the school curriculum is actually getting dumbed down in many places. This is especially and disturbingly true for schools dealing with working-class children, poor and immigrant kids, and kids of color. By contrast, the work of progressive elementary and high schools have over recent decades given us wonderful examples in the arts, drama, literacy, science, environmental studies, and mathematics of what it might look like to have children actually participate in and experience intellectual life. High schools, like Central Park East Secondary and the Urban Academy in New York, and elementary schools like Mission Hill in Boston, stand as models of education for citizenship and sophisticated thinking. They help us see a complex and sophisticated vision of educational standards at work.

4. This brings me to the final and most important way in which the democratic progressive tradition in education and politics speaks to us today. The radical, growing inequalities of power and wealth in U.S. society are harshly reflected in current school inequalities—and even, alas, in the reform efforts to reduce inequality. Now more than ever we need to link democratic possibilities in education to fresh possibilities in politics and our national life. Within education, democracy has to mean not only the participation of all children intellectually and socially in school subjects, but also a renewed fight for equal access and racial justice. We need a fresh new struggle to equalize the scandal of unequal funding for education, and new scrutiny of the role of schools in reinforcing inequalities of class and race and gender. It is also obvious that schools alone cannot take us to a better democracy, though clearly they have a role to play. Progress in education on a large scale will not happen without parallel democratic gains in the rest of U.S. society—in child care, adequate preschooling, full funding for Head Start, medical care for all families, adequate housing, full employment, voting and political and campaign finance reform, human rights, and other big steps toward a less radically unequal society. Without democratic movements to counterbalance corporate power and greed, the country will continue to move in seriously wrong directions, and teachers in public schools will continue to be scapegoats. With a sense of the true complexity of the nation's educational and social agenda, a slogan like "Leave No Childhood Behind" can be our inspiration. Without it, the slogan can become a slick joke on the rest of us.

A few threads link the many varieties of progressive practice over the centuries. They fuse the democratic ideal with the discovery of childhood and the potential for children to grow through experience—the progressive tradition offers today's rising generation of teachers and parents the adventure of the big idea that an education suited to children's nature is possible, that classrooms for everybody's children can provide opportunities for intelligent conversation and reflection on experiences that matter—and that such reflection is childhood's best preparation for both life and citizenship. Progressives from Dewey and DuBois to teachers in Reggio Emilia, Italy, today have shown such teaching to be possible with all sorts of children in many different countries and at different times in history. On the other hand, the progressive tradition at this moment in our public life also speaks with what F. Scott Fitzgerald is reported to have called "the authority of failure." Progressive, democratic ideas are not exactly in fashion today in a country whose government claims to favor democracy abroad, but not at home—and certainly not in classrooms. That is why we democratic progressives believe these ideas are needed now more than ever.

4

Teaching by the Book(s)

ALICE SELETSKY

I have read a lot of books about teaching and learning during my thirty-five years as a teacher. I bought some and borrowed others; reread the important ones, and passed them along to friends; discarded the ones I disagreed with. By midcareer, my bookshelves bulged; when I retired, I cleared away most of the books.

When the subject of this chapter came up, I began creating a list in my head of the books that had mattered most. Many titles popped right up with little prompting, like icons on my computer screen. They were such an important part of my personal history, inextricably bound up with the kind of teacher I became.

Jonathan Kozol's *Death at an Early Age* (1967) tells of the struggles for integrated schools in Boston. As far as my husband and I were concerned, the timing of its publication was exactly right. In 1964, there was a full-blown school crisis in New York City. Kozol's work was more than just another politically powerful and timely book: It was a call to arms in the integration wars.

We were living in the Bronx, where I taught in a school not far from home, and my daughters attended the local elementary school. Its racial composition reflected the immediate neighborhood, which was mostly working class and about 50 percent white, the remaining students evenly divided between Latino and black. A few blocks away was another elementary school whose population was almost entirely black and Latino. The Princeton Plan was proposed as a way to achieve a greater degree of integration. All the five- to eight-year-olds would attend one school; the nine- to twelve-year-olds the other. Our Parents Association got caught up in a fierce, divisive struggle, some of us actively advocating for the plan and

47

others very much opposed. The opposition won, the plan was scratched, and some parents stopped speaking to one another.

Jonathan Kozol gave voice to our feelings. We were impassioned and enraged, as he was, about the inequities inherent in the school system. We believed, as he did, that integrated schools would lead to equality for everyone and profound social change. Though we had lost the vote, we comforted ourselves with the thought that however bad our schools might be, they weren't as bad as Boston's.

Almost twenty years later, Kozol turned his passionate attention to a school in the South Bronx and described his experiences in *Savage Inequalities* (1991). Most of us had moved on to other struggles. Integration was no longer an issue because there were not enough white students to integrate with in our corner of the Bronx. In addition, most schools were overcrowded, understaffed, poorly maintained, and underfunded. The Bronx, it would seem, was every bit as bad as Boston had been.

The school at which I began my teaching career in the mid-sixties had once been considered a "silk stocking" school in a solidly working-class neighborhood. Some of the older staff members remembered its glory days when parents would try to enroll their ineligible children using false addresses. When I was hired to teach Class 4-2, there were ten or twelve classes of each grade, half-day kindergartens, and double sessions for first and second graders.

I was, of course, poorly trained and inexperienced; my classroom, like many others, often verged on chaos. But many books about teaching and learning were being published. These were not the canonical works by Froebel, Pestolozzi, Montessori, and company, but writings by teachers about their students and their classrooms. I turned to them with desperation and hope.

George Dennison's was a calm, unhurried voice, offering possibility and encouragement. "The business of a school," he said, "is not, or should not be mere instruction, but the life of the child" (1969, 10). I was very much reassured by the fact that some of the scenes in *The Lives of Children* were not so different from what went on in Class 4-2. I learned from Dennison how to see individual children and how to think about them. Some of the children in my class were much like Maxine and Willard and José in the First Street School. I knew I was not teaching them well, but Dennison's stories persuaded me that if I was attentive enough, I could learn to recognize, understand, and reach them. With luck, I could even teach them successfully. It was only after I reread *The Lives of Children* recently that I realized Dennison gave me another way of looking. I wouldn't have found it without him.

Teaching was difficult, often thankless, work in those first years. The children would not listen, the teachers were disheartened and harsh, and the "system" did not seem to care. It was easy for me to fall into a pattern of grinding my teeth and thinking evil thoughts as I boarded the bus and headed home at the end of each day. When I felt particularly overwhelmed, I turned the pages of *The Way It Spozed to Be* (1968) and allowed James Herndon to lighten my load with wisdom and humor. He was obviously serious and thoughtful and deeply committed to his students, but he also recognized that a little detachment and irony could go a long way toward maintaining sanity and even, surprisingly, enjoying the kids. He had his Opal who exercised her "plop reflex" when she didn't get her way; I had my Anthony who climbed to the top of the coat closet, some twelve inches from the ceiling, and crouched there like a tiger preparing to pounce.

Does anybody still read A. S. Neill? When I read him for the first time forty years ago, I found him to be an authentic educational radical (some of us were impressed by those things at the time), and I very much admired his uncompromising positions. But between that first reading and a second recent one, I had become an experienced teacher and an advocate for progressive education. I found a number of Neill's ideas unacceptable, particularly his assumption that so many of the students at Summerhill had serious emotional problems. I had forgotten his unwavering faith in Freud and his use of the word *cure*, which I found offensive, to describe the work he did with particular children.

But I can't write him off altogether because I rediscovered something that gave me great pleasure: the "examinations" he made up for the twelve-year-olds who demanded to be tested. Here is a sample question:

Where are the following: Madrid, Thursday Island, yesterday,
love, democracy, hate, my pocket screwdriver? (Neill 1960, 6)

Wouldn't it be nice, in this era of test madness, for children to be asked to take similar "examinations"? Could we make it a condition of employment that the classroom teacher make up the questions, the school principal administer it, and the Chancellor do the grading?

By the early seventies, I had gained confidence as a teacher, but I was dissatisfied with my teaching. The classroom Dewey describes in *The School and Society* was the image in my head—children doing real things such as carding wool and spinning thread, studying the ecology of seashores, hatching butterflies. What I saw, instead, each time I walked into my classroom was ". . . rows of ugly desks placed in geometrical order, crowded together so that there shall be as little moving room as possible, desks all of the same size with just space enough to hold books, pencils, and paper . . ." (1915, 31). I was experienced enough to recognize that despite my best efforts to enrich the dry, lifeless curriculum with singing, sewing, art projects, and plays, my classroom was not the kind of place that challenged and stimulated children to learn and grow.

But change was in the air, and what Dewey called the *new education* in 1915 was being revived, at least in some places. It was called, variously, British Infant School, the Integrated Day, Corridor Program, Open Education. Those of us who were exploring some of these alternatives to traditional classrooms came to know one another in college courses, workshops, and conferences. After a time, we formed supportive networks through connections to Lillian Weber's Workshop Center at City College, and to Community Resources Institute directed by Ann Cook and Herb Mack.

I started to love reading from the moment I held the first pre-primer in my hands and learned about Dick and Jane and Spot and Puff. Some of my fourth graders hated to read because it was such a struggle for them—most had a take-it-or-leave-it attitude; and only a few fluent readers were passionate about books. I wanted them all to read well and love books. I embarked on an ongoing quest for how.

Sylvia Ashton-Warner's 1963 book, *Teacher,* taught me more about literacy than anything else I had learned up to that point. I was so excited by her ideas that I tried to adapt "organic" reading and writing to the needs of my struggling fourth graders. In one form or other, "key vocabulary," word cards, dictated stories in the children's own language became elements in all my teaching. Another source of ideas and inspiration was the work of Connie and Harold Rosen whose 1973 book, *The Language of Primary School Children,* demonstrated the range and depth of what real children said and wrote and read.

One of my all-time favorites was *Wally's Stories* (1981), Vivian Paley's description of the work she did with her kindergartners. That and many of the books that followed left me awed and more than a little jealous. Like her, I was an active teacher in an active classroom, reflecting on and sometimes writing about my practice and my students. I consoled myself with the thought that her children were younger than mine, so we had different stories to tell. But I wanted to bring to my own teaching and writing what I admired in her: respectful attention, careful observation, thoughtful description.

I have left out too many books and writers whose work enriched and informed my teaching life. But I can't omit Sybil Marshall; I don't remember how or where I first discovered her, but she became indispensable. I came upon her book, *An Experiment in Education* (1963), at a time when everything we think of as essential classroom materials was in such short supply as to be virtually nonexistent. I'm talking about things like paper, crayons, glue, scissors. Clearly, Sybil understood what that meant. She recommended paper mosaic, using colored advertising pages from old magazines, cut into small pieces and glued to create forms, textures, depth . . . Magic! Shellacked and mounted, they were impressive. Put together to form a large mural titled "Animals of Africa" and displayed on the wall outside our classroom, they were dazzling.

I find it interesting that, after all these years, a handful of books stand out because they offered something I needed at a particular time in my teaching life. I suppose I could have managed without them, but I am grateful that I found them (or they found me) and that we lived happily together for so many years.

5

The School in Rose Valley

EDITH KLAUSNER

My Beginnings in Rose Valley

It has been more than two decades since I became head of The School in Rose Valley. Yet I remember so clearly getting out of my car that first time in the somewhat scruffy parking lot, looking about and thinking, "Yes, I can do this!" Much of my vision was embodied there.

An almost hidden road leads into the school. You have to watch for it... once over the rutted lane, small things stand out. They all have to do with the children. Tiny spaces, private spots that kids designed for themselves—a hidden corner near the sheep shed, or a bushy plot near the preschool. Sheep and goats roamed the grounds at various times and children accepted them as part of the daily scene, basketball hoops were forever falling down, and kids made up new games when the weather changed.

The seasons flavored much of what we did. We celebrated them in our own traditional ways. Early fall brought apple day—picking and baking and eating, with the whole school involved. We had Grandparents Day and kids were thrilled to have grandparents or friends for whom they could display their latest achievements. Our May Fair was a bright spot of dancing and games and food and visitors. The kids loved showing their school on that first real day of spring. We walked in the woods to learn more about what grew there and what we remembered from the last time. As kids grew, they remembered that one of the islands in the creek had seemed so far away just a few years ago! We had bird walks early in the morning with pancakes fried on open fires. (Every year we frantically searched for where we had put away the fire grates last year.) We sweetened the pancakes with our own home-made maple syrup. (We had such a tiny bit, but it really went far!) Kite Day happened as a surprise on a windy hill. When the wind was right, the children quickly fashioned kites and we all took off. The staff variety show amazed adults and kids alike with its inventiveness. And there was Bead Day to celebrate the year's end. Teachers took great pains to choose a special bead for that day for each child in the class, and to write a single line or two on an accompanying card to describe the child. The bead and the special words were given to each child in a little envelope. The whole school was honored and children carefully kept those beads. They appeared on their necks each year on successive Bead Days, right up until graduation. No tests on these events, just precious memories that stayed with children and families, warming their hearts long after the days passed.

Indeed children wrote and drew about these memories; they talked about the plans and then what had occurred. Various groups often had themes, such as a country that seemed exotic, like Japan, or a period of history, like Colonial times. Biographies were very popular and children worked hard to research their characters, costumes, and sometimes even foods. Children became the persons of their choice, sometimes for months or weeks. Sometimes groups created plays or wrote poetry especially for the class theme. At other times a traditional Shakespearean play was presented with great fanfare, and invitations went out to one and all to come and see and often taste what had been so thoughtfully crafted.

At The School in Rose Valley children and teachers went deeply into all plans and aspects of the school year. These held them fast, and created community. Sometimes it would be a few small groups in a classroom, sometimes a whole class got involved. Nothing was too difficult, from building a house in the woods to crafting miniature furniture for doll houses. Children learned as they were ready, with help when or if it was needed. A child might "take off" in math and be a bit less facile in reading or writing or vice versa. But it usually worked out, especially when parents felt comfortable with what The School was doing. Adults watched closely and looked carefully at what else a child was doing, what might be an extra motivating factor. It was up to The School to keep families involved, to let them know where their child's strengths were. Children's special skills were valued—music or observational skills, art or dramatic skills, scientific skills for research and analysis. And everyone loved what each was able to do.

There were, of course, troubles—this was a school of human beings after all, of barbs and tempers as well as of friendship and caring. Sometimes there were relationship issues—children who just couldn't hit it off with one another, or a particular child who managed to rub others the wrong way. Sometimes teachers didn't feel the teacher who came before (or after) them was pulling her or his own weight. Sometimes the Board, which was composed of mainly parents of students at the school, got to an impasse and it was close to impossible to get them to come to consensus. But as I look back, overall it was the caring and the concerns that we most valued and remembered.

So in what do I rejoice as I look back? The deep fun we all had. The things children remembered for long stretches, the authenticity of work plunged into with genuine appetite. Families and community were central to everything we did. Somehow parents, guardians, and relatives found time to help out despite their busy schedules. Some parents had unique gifts to share and often shared them gladly. Parents and friends were always welcome; teachers were available, as was the principal. Even during harried times, a warmth and gentleness blanketed us.

Emblematic of my personal work at The School in Rose Valley was my office with its small hard-to-work window looking out at a part of the campus, and a door that stayed open most of the time to welcome parents, teachers, children—sometimes folks burst in breathlessly, sometimes solemnly, usually glad to share the latest happening or plans. (When I retired, the Board gave me a painting entitled "Edie's Open Door." I hadn't realized it in all those years, but my door was indeed open often, and I loved whatever came through it—mostly.) Some might say that the small details weren't what my job was about. But I would disagree. They are what I remember more than the major crises and complexities. What did it matter of wars and adventures, of dates, and of famous persons? Of course it mattered. Often exciting ideas were born and researched, written of and wondered about. But in the final picture, such matters can always be retrieved in books and papers, on the Internet. Human relations and interior questions that live on can only take root in the heart.

Just opposite my office window was a very old and decrepit birdbath, which somehow became—every spring—a "potion vessel." The water that gathered in it was incredibly muddy and yucky, and certain kids adored it! Usually it became the "property" of a particular group of children—about third or fourth graders. They spent entire recesses fashioning the most "poisonous" drink they could concoct, though only from what was found outdoors: seed pods, grasses, stones, rotted leaves, flowers. Invariably these concoctions were somehow destroyed almost nightly and the following day, amidst lamentation, kids rebuilt their mixtures with tremendous intensity. Sometimes they worked together, sometimes separately, but always clearly following some "secret" plan to make an even better mixture this time.

What drew my eye and my wonder to the potion mixtures time and time again? Why did kids do this work year after year? No one told them as far as I knew what was needed there. Yet, no year was missed. It became one of those traditions that blossomed regularly with the spring, just as delighted sledding emerged on snowy days. Clearly it was about community, about finding solidarity with others to some aspect of hidden tradition, weaving and sending messages over many years.

The Way to Rose Valley

When I got to Rose Valley, I had been in education for some time. Who was I? I started teaching when I was young. (I saw it as a good job that allowed me to have the same hours and vacations as my three young kids.) But as time went on, I realized how much was embraced by the particular kinds of teaching I wanted to do. My vision grew. I had no formal training – my college career was quite checkered, but I finally got a degree, long after I was entrenched in the world of education and after some years at another progressive school. What had shaped me over those several decades? I had taught preschool and elementary grades at the school my children attended, The Miquon School, mainly under the creative tutelage of Donald and Lore Rasmussen. I worked in the Follow Through program with Ernestine Rouse, Marie Tervalon, David Armington, George Hein, and many other skillful folk.

At that time we had a Teacher Center (The District Six Advisory Center), which contributed greatly to my understanding of what teachers were thinking and asking about education in those days. The Center attracted many heroes and heroines of progressive education at that time, great names and modest ones—teachers who taught around the corner or at some distance, parents who knew they were welcome and loved to come and hang out. All who came recognized something that spoke to them. All shared some part of a larger vision that was growing and being nurtured in those days. I loved meeting with our staff and tailoring the programs and the spaces for teachers and others who might learn what mattered to them in our shop and workrooms. No one checked to see whether what they did at the Teacher Center had an impact, a score, an influence in their classrooms or schools. (We were privately funded and the funders seemed to trust our work.) Learning at the Center was rather like that scene at the birdbath, making me wonder what teachers had in mind. I knew that the effort had a purpose, even if I couldn't see it right off.

Other threads were woven in. During these years, I had visited and been visited by Lillian Weber and Deborah Meier from New York; Eleanor Duckworth from Boston; and Patricia Carini and her staff at the Prospect Center and School from North Bennington, Vermont. I worked with Ted Chittenden, Anne Bussis, and Marianne Amarel of Educational Testing Service in Princeton, along with Philadelphia public school teachers, on a study of how children learn to read. I learned a great deal from those teachers and their students as well as from the ETS researchers.

After our Center sadly closed in the late seventies (private funding ended and the local district was unwilling to see it continue), some of us formed the Philadelphia Teachers' Learning Cooperative, which meets to this day (some thirty continuous years), to discuss children and school issues, community, and identity. I attended yearly meetings of the North Dakota Study Group on Evaluation that was led by Vito Perrone of Harvard University. At those meetings there were many influences and much fellowship and more and more ideas about how to try to make good things happen for kids. I heard speakers and saw the leadership of Hubert Dyasi, Joseph Suina, and Richard Gray. I read the work of Jay Featherstone, Herbert Kohl, Mike Rose, and so many others, and each time I would think, "Yes!" And perhaps I would understand a bit more. Much from that time is knitted into my head.

Looking Back

It is now a decade since I left The School in Rose Valley. When I return to visit, I see that The School is a good deal more spiffed up with neat paths and a beautiful new all-purpose building—yet the feeling of friendly community, inclusiveness, and risk-taking remains. When I first arrived, The School had fallen on hard times—these small schools tend to do that. But its Board of parents and teachers was determined to pull through and they were looking hard for someone who was willing to work for not too much money and put lots of energy into its resurgence. That person turned out to be me. I learned way more than I taught.

I am always learning. Even in writing this chapter, I am learning more about what matters, what influenced me, what must be gathered further into the web of life, the web of children's lives as they go on. In spite of government mandates, children's lives have a central core of trust and interest in the world, and if allowed they will live by it. We had a favorite song at our weekly sing gathering, Joni Mitchell's "Circle Game." The song says "We're captive on the carousel of time" and "can only look behind from where we came." We do look behind quite regularly. And we learn from that. At least I do.

PART TWO

Education and Democracy

This part begins with an overview of the recent history of public educational policy. Harold Berlak relates how progressive educational ideas and practices have fared since the mid-sixties; how control has been gradually taken over as a result of the federal government imposing various forms of standardization—prescribed methods, texts, content, and expectations—that have been reinforced by a complicit standardized tests industry.

In an example of effective education for democracy, Francisco Guajardo describes a strong community-based initiative in South Texas. He introduces four first-person accounts by Mexican-American youth that show the power of storytelling (recorded oral histories) in bringing about the kind of consciousness that can lead to individual and group change.

Turning to the internal politics of the North Dakota Study Group itself, Hollee Freeman, an eye-witness, examines its positive influence on its members and, at the same time, its difficulties exemplifying some of the principles and values it espouses

Finally, Connie Henry weighs the advantages and disadvantages of public versus private education in terms of social responsibility. A public school advocate while teaching in a private school, Henry makes a case for all educational institutions to share responsibility for more progressive, worthwhile, democratic education.

6

Education Policy 1964–2004
The No Child Left Behind Act and the Assault on Progressive Education and Local Control

HAROLD BERLAK

As a progressive and teacher, I hold two interconnected sets of values and beliefs. The first is pedagogical and curricular—ways of viewing human development; childhood; adolescence; and the nature of learning, knowledge, and knowing. Progressive practices aim to engage the learner; to nurture imagination and cognitive and artistic expression; and to foster social–emotional and moral development. The words most often associated with such practices are *whole child* and *child-centered*. While these terms oversimplify, they encapsulate core values of the progressive pedagogical tradition.

The second set is political and addresses the question of control—how power is distributed throughout society including schools, and the role of government at all levels. At the core of political progressivism is a commitment to, or perhaps more aptly, an aspiration for democracy—that there should not be a hierarchy of privilege based on wealth, status, race, gender; and everyone should be able to exercise their basic human rights including the right to participate fully in making decisions that affect our lives and the life of our communities. This includes control over the institutions that educate the young. I believe democracy requires economic and social equality, the redistribution *down* of money, power, cultural capital, pleasure, and freedom.

In the next several pages, I address how these two pillars of progressive education, the pedagogical and political, have fared over the years, from the mid-sixties and early seventies—the period that gave rise in 1972 to convening what came to be called the North Dakota Study Group on Evaluation—through today, the age of "compassionate conservatism."

The Rise and Fall of the "Great Society"

In accepting the nomination for president in 1960, John F. Kennedy spoke of a "New Frontier"—a "frontier of unfulfilled hopes;" and as president, he would address the ". . . unsolved problems of peace and war, unconquered pockets of ignorance and prejudice, unanswered questions of poverty." However, at the time of his assassination in 1963, most New Frontier proposals were marooned in a Congress dominated by an alliance of pro-corporate Republicans and avowedly racist, Southern Democrats adamantly opposed to the implementation of the 1954 Brown v. Board of Education desegregation decision. When Lyndon Johnson assumed office, he embraced the idealism of the New Frontier and in a commencement address at the University of Michigan in May 1964, spoke eloquently about what he called the "Great Society." It is a humane and inclusive vision of American democracy, and of a government dedicated to protecting civil rights and liberties and serving social justice.

> The Great Society rests on abundance and liberty for all. It demands an end to poverty and racial injustice, to which we are totally committed in our time. But that is just the beginning.
>
> The Great Society is a place where every child can find knowledge to enrich his [sic] mind and to enlarge his talents. It is a place where leisure is a welcome chance to build and reflect, not a feared cause of boredom and restlessness. It is a place where the city of man serves not only the needs of the body and the demands of commerce but the desire for beauty and the hunger for community. (*Public Papers*, 1965, 704–7)

During the next two years, former Texas Senator Johnson, Democratic majority leader and consummate deal maker, navigated through a recalcitrant Congress an impressive array of progressive laws and programs unrivaled since the early New Deal. These included the 1965 Civil Rights Act to outlaw racial discrimination in public accommodations and voter registration; the Economic Opportunity Act, which established the OEO (Office of Economic Opportunity) along with Job Corps, remedial and vocational education programs, work–study grants for students, and VISTA—a domestic peace corps; a revision of the Immigration and Nationality Act, which repealed the notorious system of racist national quotas imposed in the 1920s; the Voting Rights Act, which put teeth into the enforcement of the twenty-fourth Amendment to the Constitution ratified a year earlier; Medicare and Medicaid; the Federal Housing Act; and the Clean Air and Water Act. The list goes on.

In 1965 Johnson's two landmark educational initiatives were unveiled: Head Start and the Elementary and Secondary Education Act (ESEA). Head

Start was conceived in 1964 as a prekindergarten day-care program by a panel convened by OEO that was composed of fourteen nationally prominent experts on children's health, social and cognitive development, and childhood education. The goal of Head Start was to "break the cycle of poverty" by providing poor children and their families with a comprehensive program to address a wide range of needs—physical and emotional health, socialization, nutrition, and education. It began as an eight-week summer program in 1965 with a few thousand children and by 2004 grew to a $7 billion annual program serving just over 900,000 poor children in 18,000 centers located in every state, D.C., Puerto Rico, and U.S. territories.

From the perspective of policy and politics, what is striking about Head Start is how it was organized and controlled at the national and local levels. The locus of control for program design, governance, and personnel rested with the local staff and policy councils or advisories composed of parents, staff, and members of the immediate community. There was federal oversight, but little interference in personnel policies and day-to-day operations. In an effort to ensure that Head Start retains its comprehensive, holistic, balanced emphasis and not stress the academic over health and other developmental areas, the federal Head Start bureau was deliberately located outside the Office of Education (predecessor of the U.S. Department of Education), and local programs were independent of state and local school authority.

ESEA was devised to provide aid directly to local districts and schools that served children of the "disadvantaged." Its purview expanded over the years and it now authorizes funds for Indian education, teacher training, early literacy, school libraries, bilingual education, technology, and school safety. In 2004, Title I, its largest set of programs, authorized $11.7 billion of aid to 47,000, nearly half of the nation's public schools. While federal dollars account for only 7 percent of the nation's expenditures for schools, these dollars are critical to districts and schools that serve disproportionately large populations of the poor, African Americans, Latinos, and immigrants for whom English is a second language.

At the time ESEA passed, it was widely presumed that a basic value of U.S. democracy was that schooling of the young was a local community responsibility. While the states set guidelines, and provided funds and oversight, specific pedagogical and curricular decisions were mostly left to teachers, principals, districts, and locally elected governing boards. There were exceptions, notably the textbook adoption states—California, Texas, and several states in the deep South. But even these states lacked the legal mandate and/or the bureaucratic apparatus to force compliance to specific curricular and pedagogical mandates. To guard against intrusions by "federal officials, Congress added explicit language to ESEA prohibiting any federal agency or official from exercising direction, supervision, or control over the curriculum, program of instruction, administration, or personnel in any educational institution or school system." Most ESEA funds went directly to local authorities, thereby bypassing the authority of the states' education officials and departments of education.

In 1967, the final piece of the Great Society educational agenda was set in place. Called "Follow Through," it was intended to capitalize on progress made by Head Start by providing educational services to children from kindergarten through third grade. However, by 1967, talk of the Great Society and the War on Poverty had all but disappeared from mainstream politics; 1965 was the zenith of Great Society legislative accomplishment, but it was also a year of other fateful events that led to the unraveling of the Johnson presidency. Thousands of "advisors" and massive U.S. bombings had failed to secure victory in Vietnam and Johnson dispatched the first contingent of combat troops—3,500 Marines—to Vietnam in early March. By year's end, there were 184,000 troops there and the numbers were rising. As the numbers swelled, so too did antiwar protests on college campuses across the country. The resistance was widespread and was led by a new generation of radical (largely white male) college students, known collectively as the "New Left."

The year 1965 was also a time of domestic violence and racial ferment. There were civil rights demonstrations and marches throughout the South led by Martin Luther King Jr. and the Southern Christian Leadership Council. Coincidentally, the first contingent of Marines arrived in Vietnam on the Monday following "Bloody Sunday"—a day when peaceful marchers in Selma were gassed and brutally beaten by Alabama state troopers in plain sight of cameras and the national press. Also in 1965 several thousand young men and women descended on the South to test the Johnson Administration's resolve to make good on its vow to defend civil rights. It was during the same year that Malcolm X was assassinated while preaching a message of black unity and resistance (as opposed to nonviolence); and that Watts, a neighborhood of the desperately poor in Los Angeles—mostly African American and Latino—erupted into six days of uncontrolled violence that killed 34, wounded 1,000, burned and leveled hundreds of buildings, and led to the arrest and jailing of more than 4,000. From 1965 through 1967, the first full year of Project Follow Through, there was violence in 100 cities across the United States. King delivered his historic sermon, "A Time to Break Silence," at the New York City Riverside Church in 1967; it forged a link between antiwar and civil rights movements.

In the competition for guns or butter, the guns again won. As the costs of the war soared, Great Society programs were funded at a fraction of projected costs. Project Follow Through was originally intended to aid *all* public elementary schools serving the poor at a cost estimated at just over a billion dollars annually. It was funded in the tens of millions, less than 10 percent of the original estimate. In March 1968, the "Tet offensive"—the simultaneous attack on U.S.-held cities and military installations across Vietnam—punctured the myth that a U.S. victory was at hand. Johnson's popularity plummeted to a new low, nearing 30 percent. With the national election on the horizon, a disheartened, unpopular Johnson shocked the nation by his announcement that he would not seek another term. Later that same year, the two icons of the growing antiwar and civil rights movements—Martin Luther King Jr. and Robert F. Kennedy—were murdered, and in November Richard Nixon was elected president on a platform of restoring fiscal responsibility and pursuing "peace with honor."

It is important to note how Project Follow Through managed to survive until 1994. It was rationalized as an "experiment" to test and to establish once and for all which of the approaches taken by the two dozen or so project sponsors was the most effective. Use of standardized tests for this purpose sparked strong opposition at the Denver 1972 meeting of Follow Through directors, precipitating the convening of the group of progressive educators in Grand Forks hosted by Vito Perrone, later named the North Dakota Study Group on Evaluation (see this book's introduction by Brenda Engel). It is ironic that this tactical ploy aimed at saving Follow Through by converting it to an experiment not only contributed to the program's demise but also it marked the first time the federal government employed standardized testing as the primary measure of educational success.

The Right-Wing Counterrevolution

The decade of the sixties and escalation of the Vietnam War were accompanied by massive political, social, and cultural transformations. Social conventions and authority—family, corporate, government, and university —were everywhere under siege or so it appeared to those in power. This tumultuous decade gave birth to a new assertive black identity movement that demanded not only civil and voting rights but also political and economic power; a progressive antiwar movement able to drive a president from office; a reinvigorated women's movement; and consumer and environmental protection movements foreshadowing others—La Raza, Native American, Asian American, and gay rights among them. The fears that the sixties' movements provoked in the halls of government, big business, and culturally right-wing sectors of American society are difficult to exaggerate. As the 1970s began, the major U.S. corporations were experiencing what the business pages call a "profit squeeze." The World War II U.S. enemies, Germany and Japan, were seriously challenging the economic dominance of the United

States. All moves toward liberal, social democracy that would restrict corporate power were portrayed by its leaders as serious threats to corporate profitability, economic recovery, and growth. To Christian fundamentalists the cultural transformations of the sixties were a frontal assault by the godless on their cherished values and beliefs about family, sexuality, and patriotism.

Nixon's election confirmed the beginnings of a successful counter-revolution orchestrated by an (uneasy) alliance between U.S. financial corporate interests and the far right aimed at undoing the social, political, and legal gains of the Great Society and the New Deal, and devaluing diversity. Now, more than thirty years later, this coalition of shared interests is in full command of the leadership of the Republican Party, the Congress, and the Supreme Court. They maneuvered the election of a president who calls himself a compassionate conservative and decries big government while unabashedly using the power of government to promote corporate interests, increase the wealth of the wealthiest, undermine civil and women's rights, and suppress dissent. A major locus for the consolidation of state power and extending corporate influence is education, preschool through the university.

While ESEA and Head Start survived, there were changes over the years that eroded by increments the historic commitment to democratic community control of schools. Bush, the elder, called the first "educational summit" in 1989. It was dominated by Fortune 500 corporate executives, governors, and federal officials who concluded national standardized testing is essential for federal and state officials to exercise control of curriculum, teaching and learning, and teacher qualifications. Their proposal for national testing failed to make it though Congress. Bush's successor, Bill Clinton, the "New Democrat" and champion of national testing, managed to get his "Goals 2000" Act through Congress. Among other things this legislation authorized grants to states to develop assessments that linked so-called *content* standards to standardized testing. But Clinton's proposal for national testing died in Congress because of the opposition of the Black Caucus and Christian fundamentalists led by then Senator John Ashcroft.

Where Clinton and Bush Sr. failed, George W. Bush was successful. He attached his proposal for national testing to the 2001 revision of ESEA, and rechristened it the No Child Left Behind Act. The law cedes unprecedented powers to federal officials. As a condition of receiving federal dollars, states must now adopt content standards linked to standardized testing; and schools must measure and make "Annual Yearly Progress"—as determined by federal regulations. All curriculum materials and services for teaching reading (and soon math) must be approved in advance as "scientifically based;" and all school staff must be "highly qualified" as defined by federal regulations that nullify local prerogatives and state law. To gain the votes of conservative Republicans in Congress who are ideologically opposed to federal intervention and national testing, Bush tacked on two provisions. One requires all public schools receiving federal dollars to provide student lists to military recruiters. The second mandates that no school or district can deny the Boy Scouts, or any other group listed as a "patriotic society" under the U.S. Code, access to school facilities for after-school meetings even if this violates state and local antidiscrimination statutes.

The Future of a New Progressive Education Movement

Tactical moves by the right thus undermined much of the Great Society, turning the nation's historic commitment to local control on its head. They framed the issues of school reform in terms of raising standards and measuring results and promoted the fiction that gains in standardized test scores and the improvement of academic standards are one and the same. Billions of corporate dollars over the last fifteen years have created a vast new generation of think tanks, foundations, and nonprofits, which produce reports and studies to buttress right-wing, pro-corporate policies and discount evidence that right-wing policies deny opportunities and widen gender, class, and race inequalities. The school curriculum is controlled by a No Child Left Behind Act provision, which requires that all teaching materials and services be "scientifically based" thereby eliminating materials and approaches that don't fit the right-wing education agenda. The right, in an intellectual coup, rewrote the history of the sixties, casting the Great Society programs as failures and the social movements of the times as the enemies of progress, prosperity, and the common good, while celebrating the Republican Party as true defenders of freedom and equality.

In my view, if a new unified progressive education movement is to emerge as a force in U.S. politics, it must capture the initiative, reasserting for the twenty-first century the fundamental political and pedagogical values of progressive education. We must acknowledge the need for public accountability in terms of careful, open recordkeeping and local, curriculum-related tests; and at the same time, directly challenge *all* forms of national and statewide standardized testing used singly or in conjunction with other measures to rank schools, define achievement or merit, or distribute rewards and sanctions to schools and teachers. Substituting the current crop of standardized tests with a new breed of "authentic" standardized tests is not an advance because they do not challenge the centralization of power. Standardized testing is the key issue because it is the essential tool for centralizing control. Without standardized tests, top-down, bureaucratic government control of teaching and learning cannot function.

It is vital that progressive educators reclaim the history of progressivism and progressive education in the United States, not only to discredit the rampant right-wing mythology but also to renew their own understanding of, and learn from, its pedagogical and political successes and failures. Many progressive educators depoliticized progressive education, viewing it narrowly as a children's rights and pedagogical movement to the exclusion of a wider vision of economic and political democracy. If a new reinvigorated national progressive education movement is to take shape, it must see itself also as a political movement, as an integral part of the broader struggle for human rights, social and economic justice. And progressive educators must deal with cultural parochialism, classism, and racism within our practices and organizations. These are deeply rooted in history and remain as formidable barriers to collective action and achieving democracy and equality.

7

Narratives of Transformation
Education and Social Change in Rural South Texas

FRANCISCO GUAJARDO
AND THE LLANO GRANDE CENTER STUDENTS

The Llano Grande Center for Research and Development met the North Dakota Study Group in the summer of 1997, when teachers and students from Edcouch-Elsa High School (E-E High) in South Texas came upon Vito Perrone. Vito directed the Annenberg Rural Challenge Evaluation team, and I directed the nascent Llano Grande Center, which was born out of my classroom at E-E High—a rural public high school located along the Texas-Mexico border (see Figure 7–1). We described Llano Grande's purpose as an attempt to capture the story of a community through the use of a range of activities in our public schools. We would build relationships with elders as we collected their experiences through oral histories; our students and teachers would become active participants in building the history of our community. Equally important, we suggested to Vito that as our students listened to the stories of the elders, the students themselves would emerge as storytellers.

Vito was intrigued by this notion. "Tell me more about that, about young people becoming storytellers," he asked.

"Well, Vito, we're not quite sure how that's going to happen, but I know we're committed to the process. Let's wait and see," I said.

Students as Ethnographers

Shortly after our conversation, the center embarked on a community-based research project where we trained student ethnographers to conduct oral histories, write reflective journals, and work on creating digital stories focused on their lives as youths in rural South Texas. Hundreds of E-E High

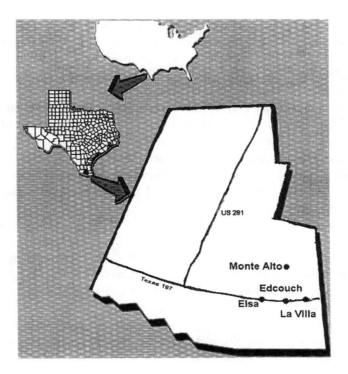

Figure 7–1

students took part in the ethnography research project, and each took seriously the act of interviewing, self-reflecting, and building a community history. In the end, the ethnography project helped students understand themselves and their personal, familial, and community identities. The following student reflections convey some of that understanding.

Myrta Ventura

Through studying her family's story, Myrta Ventura found there was no shame in her experience as a migrant farmworker. Herein, she describes her struggles and her triumphs.

Edcouch, Texas, is the only place that I can truly call home, but as a migrant, it is not the only place I live in. Every year as school comes to an end and the heat begins to burn, my family packs our bags and boards up our house. It would be nice to say that leaving gets easier every year, but I cannot. It has gotten tougher every year. I can't say goodbye to my friends because I'm not really leaving, and I can't get sad because I know that I'll be back. Sometimes the only thing you can do is close your eyes for five minutes, because that is how long it takes to leave Edcouch and Elsa. Then, when you open your eyes, all you can do is hope that the three months of upcoming labor will speed by.

I can honestly say that up until my twelfth year of life I did not know what work was. Then one morning before the sun rose, my mother shook me out of bed and told me to get up. It was time to work. I didn't take the moment seriously because it was summer, and I was still twelve. No one under twenty woke up before the sun, especially when you didn't have school. Who was I to break this unspoken rule? Unfortunately, that did not pass through my parents' minds.

The moment initiated my new stage of life, as a worker. I was to rise at the same time as the adults, and to do the same work as the adults. So at twelve years old my summer days were going to be spent in the fields. We started off thinning peaches, the job that I hate with all of my heart. We rose at five in the morning, to make the day shorter and cooler, and terminated each day at around three. This cycle continued for the first month, and proceeded with the picking of raspberries, cherries, and blackberries for the last two months. While other kids were at home watching TV and going swimming, I was beneath the sun in my peach tree wearing long-sleeved shirts.

I did not complain as I worked because I understood that this was what my parents needed me to accept. If I complained, I would only make myself look foolish because every other person there wasn't complaining. So, every morning as I rose my heart sank, and I longed to make the sun disappear or the clouds pour their rain. My twelfth summer of life was spent in denial and confusion.

I am now eighteen, and I've gone back to Utah as a worker for the last five summers. As each summer passed, I learned things that I know other people would take a lifetime to learn. I experienced life with a new perspective, and I found myself being thankful to my parents for teaching me what hard work is. The opportunities that this type of work offers are overshadowed by society's stereotype of migrant farmworkers. Positive effects are blurred by the negative statistics and other data that researchers, the media, and others collect.

My summers spent in and with the land have educated me. I still deplore thinning peaches, but I have an understanding of life and nature that makes my heart race. Every day that I begin before the sun is to my benefit. With this teacher, I have become a better student, not only of school, but also of life.

Myrta conducted numerous oral histories, including a historic interview with her grandmother, Rosa García, who unfortunately passed away within months after the oral history—the videotape of the interview has become a prized family possession. Myrta attends Brown University in Providence, Rhode Island, and intends to pursue a Ph.D. in geology because she loves the land.

Olga Cardoso

Like many students at E-E High, Olga Cardoso came into the United States illegally. She arrived at the high school at fifteen, just three years after crossing the Rio Grande River with her family. Olga became part of the work of the Llano Grande when she founded the Llano Grande Spanish Immersion Institute in 2001. She writes about her family's struggle to survive when she lived in the Mexican border town of Las Flores.

After my family and I left Guanajuato, we settled in Nuevo Progreso, Tamaulipas, also known as Las Flores. Life in Las Flores was very difficult economically. The money my father provided was not enough to make ends meet. It was because of this that my sister and I were forced to sell paper flowers "en el centro." My mother learned how to make paper flowers from my neighbor. My sister and I would go to school from eight until noon, and after that we sold paper flowers until five o'clock. It was too humiliating at first, but I soon realized that it was no crime. I had nothing to be ashamed of; it was what I had to do to help my mom make ends meet.

I have learned to value my education. I have learned to value everything that my parents have done for me and given me. I find myself in search of answers to many of my questions. But more than anything I find myself longing to relive the beauty of my childhood.

During her senior year at E-E High, Olga Cardoso lobbied the Texas State Legislature to change its law regarding undocumented students. The state subsequently passed House Bill 1403, allowing Olga and other undocumented students access to public colleges and universities in Texas. Fortunately, Olga became a legal resident the summer after graduating from E-E High. She attends Southwestern University in Georgetown, Texas, and intends to become an immigration lawyer.

José Cruz

When José Cruz's mother was nine months pregnant and residing in the Mexican border town of Reynosa, Tamaulipas, she decided to cross the Rio Grande

River into McAllen, where she would give birth to her baby José. Three days later, she took her newborn back to Mexico, where they rejoined their family. The Cruz family eventually crossed to the United States shortly before José enrolled in middle school.

I would like to speak a little bit about my family. Although we are very poor monetarily and we lack the luxuries that other students my age may have, I have to stress that my family has had a great influence on me. Every time I speak at a national, state, or local conference, it is not I who speaks; rather, it is my father's wisdom and my mother's humility that speak. It is the laughter of my brothers and the sparks of friendship of my two sisters. It is the stories shared by my grandfather, and the struggle to live and laugh of my grandmother. Everything that I stand for, everything that I am is my family. Those are the roots of who I am and that is what I portray. It is the feelings and the *sentimiento* of my family that speak through me. I am just a vehicle through which their words are spoken.

To many people, their roots seem to be unimportant. I am glad that all of my classmates learned to value the importance of family, of their roots, and not be ashamed of who they are. As people read this, I would like to encourage them to converse with one another, to speak with their *abuelos*, their *tias o tios*, to be one with their friends and family. The importance of conversation has been a forgotten art, an art we used to practice with pride. Fortunately, I have always conversed with my parents, aunts, and uncles. The stories they tell are most valuable. It is not whether they are making up their stories, or whether they are boring. It is the history they share, and the richness of the experience of sharing that is important.

The thing I learned the most at Edcouch-Elsa High School through my work with the Llano Grande Center was learning from each other. I presented at four conferences in just one semester and learned that many people have many misconceptions. Although the conversations regarding oral histories have made me a better public speaker, what I learned most at conferences is about how differently people think. I believe that an oral history is largely about knowing how to understand each other. That is why people who do not understand each other cannot have a good conversation, or have a good oral history. We should understand the importance of one another and know that each one has a valuable history to tell.

As we are placed in this system where competition and change are introduced, unfortunately the thing we learn most is to assimilate and feel ashamed of what we have. I had always been ashamed of what I was, of what my parents owed, of the food that I ate, and of speaking the language that I speak. I don't feel that way any more. I have changed, and I believe I have also seen a change in the community in general. I credit much of my transformation to my work with the Llano Grande Center.

José attends Yale University in New Haven, Connecticut, and plans to pursue a profession in the medical field.

Cecilia Garza

Cecilia struggled through her first years at E-E High. She spent time in school suspension, was repeatedly reprimanded by school leaders, and was about to "fall through the cracks" when she found the Llano Grande Center. When she became part of the work of the center, she emerged as a leader of the community oral history project. Cecilia turned herself around and graduated from E-E High in good standing.

It wasn't until I began doing oral histories that I learned the immense value that a person's story has—even more so when I had the opportunity to interview my grandfather.

As other students and I interviewed him, it was as if I was getting a history lesson on World War II all over again, only this time I realized that my grandpa played an important role in it. I had no idea that he was part of the Normandy Invasion. I had heard of D-Day, but I never paid as much attention as I did in that interview. My grandfather has wonderful stories to tell but I never bothered to ask until then.

Since that interview, I saw my grandpa's eyes light up. He was no longer scolding me: He was acknowledging the hard work that our class was doing. Now every morning that he takes me to school we talk about the weather, about his cows, and every now and then he'll take a detour to show where the old Mexican school used to be or anything else I should know. I'm glad that now I've learned to appreciate my grandpa's words because I had always taken them for granted.

However, I did not go without punishment for my ignorance. My grandmother is no longer able to speak, so I can't talk to her the way I used to or even the new way that I learned. It's too late for those conversations; all I can do now is read the expressions on her face and reassure her that I love her. If people learn to value others' words and understand the power that the story has to strengthen relationships, perhaps they will not miss out on all the special encounters they could have had, such as with me and my grandmother.

Cecilia Garza attends Columbia University in New York City and looks forward to becoming a public school teacher.

Closing Reflection

Personal and community narratives are central to the work of the Llano Grande Center, just as narratives of transformation have been integral to the history of the North Dakota Study Group. During my first meeting with Vito in 1997, I remember he asked Orlando Castillo, one of my students, "Orlando, how have you changed as a result of your work with Llano Grande?" Orlando responded, "I have found who I am, Vito. That's how I have changed."

In the winter of 2000, Perrone invited students and teachers from the Llano Grande Center to become members of the North Dakota Study Group.

8

The Long-Term Benefits of Getting Splashed

An African-American Progressive Educator's Experience with Progressivism

HOLLEE FREEMAN

Membership in the North Dakota Study Group (NDSG) for me represented membership in an elite group of educational activists. Well-known reformers—such as Vito Perrone, Deborah Meier, Jay Featherstone, Elsa Weber, and Mara Sapon-Shevin—helped shape conversations with new educators, like me, around themes of educational change and social justice at each yearly meeting. As a third-year teacher on a mission to make my teaching meaningful for the mostly Dominican students with whom I worked, I was at home at the NDSG. I soaked up the conversations like a sponge yet always felt slightly outside of the omnipresent legacy that appeared in flesh and bones at the meetings. Still, for me, attending the NDSG as a member of the Muscota New School, a small progressive school in New York City, was emotionally and intellectually liberating. Along with the racially, culturally, and linguistically diverse group of teachers from Muscota, I found ways of translating the experiences of NDSG to my classroom of seven- and eight-year-old students.

In effect, my classroom practice was revitalized yearly. I continually focused on issues of social justice, equity, and access in each curricular area and I had a joy for teaching and learning that has since been unmatched in my professional career. Confronting issues, such as social justice, democracy in education, and progressivism, at the NDSG meetings enabled me to grow into a highly effective teacher with explicit values that I continue to maintain throughout my career. At Muscota, we engaged in child studies, reflective practice, peer review, and other activities that allowed us to see children as they are rather than as what we hope they might be. These practices were reinforced for me at the NDSG and I was grateful.

Membership was informal. You simply (or not so simply) had to know someone who was already in the group. Since the founding of the NDSG, a core group of educational activists have gotten together yearly and, as the Study Group grew, began to invite their colleagues. Although not intentional, this meant that in the year 1994 when I joined, membership was overwhelmingly comprised of older white educators and activists. Simply put, the conversations year after year focused on issues of equity and social justice in schooling, yet the group of people having these conversations was overwhelmingly racially homogeneous. I began to think about this fact from my perspective as a young, progressive, African-American educator. How could I share in the conversation? What should I say? What could I say?

I had had an ivy-league education; went to a historically progressive graduate school; and participated in professional organizations such as the Coalition of Essential Schools, the Center for Collaborative Education, the Prospect Center, and other groups with progressive educational agendas. In a sense, I was primed to participate in NDSG conversations. However, I was frequently one of the few people of color at these (or any other progressive education) meetings. I seemed to have similar ideals and educational experiences as other members of the group but hadn't found my voice there as a young urban progressive, African-American educator.

I began to ask myself questions such as: What educational networks existed and for whom? Was there an active interest in racially and culturally integrating the group? Did people of color shy away from progressive ideas? Was the lack of racial and cultural diversity really a coincidence or a pattern?

The NDSG began to actively seek more racially and culturally diverse individuals to plan meetings, to suggest speakers and panels and to develop ways to socially integrate new and more veteran members into the group. As educators from River East, El Puente, Llano Grande Center for Research and Development, as well as other, more diverse schools and community organizations, began to attend the meetings, a shift in the conversations began to occur. One particularly interesting meeting was the result of these efforts.

In 2000, there was a robust influx of new (and I might add racially and culturally diverse) members at the meeting. I specifically remember the impact of African-American teachers and Mexican-American community activists. During one of our whole-group discussions, questions and comments were raised by members of this "new" crowd that ruffled more than a few feathers of the older, more established members. I felt distinctly caught in the middle—having been in the group long enough to feel as though I was a small part of its history and yet not long enough to be bound by it. Through a debriefing of one of these conversations (during which quite a few people became frustrated, yelled, even cried), a (then)

Muscota New School teacher, Grace Schickler, put the issue into perspective for me (and I think for the whole group).

Grace likened the de facto "exclusive club nature" of the NDSG to a swimming pool. The more veteran members who spent most of their adult years nurturing the group were in the pool, happily bobbing up and down on their floats and enjoying exciting, demanding conversations. With the addition of new people to the pool, these "veterans" were splashed a bit. They got water on their faces, some felt slightly uncomfortable with the rising water level and by the introduction of tiny shifts in conversations. However, emotions quickly settled down and conversations resumed. At this point, everyone was happy in the pool. The splashing subsided, the newer folks were just happy to be in the same water with the more experienced activists, and we all continued to have meaningful conversations. I saw *my* history in this story as I remembered being new to the group and being in awe of the tremendous intellectual and philosophical gifts that resided in the people attending the meetings.

The pool metaphor continued each year as more new people attended the North Dakota Study Group. Some would wade in, some would put a toe in and gently slide into the water. In the year 2000, however, we happened to have a group of new people who liked to jump right in. Some even enjoyed doing "cannonballs" into the water; much to the chagrin of some veterans of the group. In their mind, cannonballs were devastating to the serenity of the pool and all who were within it. Some people who were in the pool fell off their floats and safety devices, some went under water, some were jumped upon. Some people actually enjoyed it and decided to join the fun. Others sauntered out, shaking their heads at the lack of respect shown for the way people entered the pool. These individuals looked back and thought nostalgically about the way it used to be and were forced to make individual choices about their ability to enjoy and be productive in this type of environment.

I personally enjoyed the cannonballs and felt a kinship to those initiating them. Yet at the same time, I felt empathy for the group of individuals who had worked tirelessly to achieve all that the NDSG stood for. For the first time, I thought of what it must be like to feel as though your future is being determined without you and without a glance to the past.

In my opinion, the introduction of cannonballs was both scary and necessary for the NDSG and has brought the group into a new era of conversation. Our conversations have become more firmly fixed on personal, racial, cultural, gender-related characteristics and how these mesh with and bump up against our individual and collective work around progressive education, social justice, and equity. In 2003, almost ten years after attending my first NDSG meeting, we were privileged to hear remarks by Vito Perrone,

Hubert Dyasi, Deborah Meier, Francisco Guajardo, Jay Featherstone, and others as they led conversations around issues of equity, access, and social justice. At this meeting, titled "Democracy, Power, and Trust," I organized a racially diverse panel of teachers to relate their personal stories and actions around issues of social justice as they apply to teaching and learning in their classrooms. In giving teachers a voice, I reinforced my own voice.

The North Dakota Study Group has a deep history in education. It has served as a catalyst for many influential events and moments in progressive education—in urban centers as well as in rural and suburban areas, in both the public and the private sector. We, as a group, have actively embraced the role of diversity and continue to add many different voices into our conversations. The group is becoming more public, trying out new ideas, and gearing up for many more years in the field of progressive education. It is my earnest belief that the goals we are pursuing in the NDSG will mean that educators and activists like myself will find their voices in conversations, in stories, and in actions so that they might transfer these voices back to classrooms, schools, and community organizations to the benefit of all the students we serve.

9

Building a Coalition
Private Schools with a Public View

CONNIE HENRY

Although I work in a private school, I consider myself essentially a public school advocate. I began my teaching career in community programs and then taught in an urban Head Start program. As long ago as that was, I can recall my first feelings of the wonder and possibility in teaching, feelings that have not dimmed as I have learned more about teaching and learning. I have been teaching and working at the Atrium School for the past twenty years. The Atrium is a small, relatively young independent school in Watertown, Massachusetts, whose mission is founded on progressive principles.

There are many of us in the private sector who participate in the North Dakota Study Group (perhaps a third of its total membership) and share its concerns about current attitudes toward teaching and learning. The tradition of the Study Group is one of dialogue and commitment to addressing the needs of all children and young people, whether in private or in public schools. However, since public education is a public responsibility, providing for the welfare of public schools in terms of adequate and equitable resources is of particularly urgent concern and is central to defining our values as a society.

What then are the commonalties and contrasts between public and private schools, particularly in relation to progressive education? While public and private progressive school educators often share a common philosophical framework, their schools clearly differ in ways that affect their ability to live by their beliefs. Examining some of the most salient differences one at a time, however, will reveal some of the interconnected advantages and disadvantages of private versus public educational institutions.

The locus of accountability and control for both models is a powerful determining factor in how well practice can align with educational missions and tenets. While the current national direction is to evaluate a child's worthiness as a student through mandated testing based on specified standards, private schools are notably exempt from these demands. There is irony in this situation. Is the government not concerned about what happens to that 10 percent of the school population?

A board of trustees is the governance structure in private schools. Its primary functions are to ensure fiscal responsibility, to create school policy, and to support (or fire) the director of the school. While the director is accountable to it, the board does not have the authority to affect daily operations and educational directions. The educational leadership of the school decides the design of the program and its methods of assessment. There is freedom from bureaucracy in terms of the hiring and firing of faculty and administrators as well. Individual schools are accredited through the regional chapters of the National Association of Independent Schools (NAIS). Indeed, the accreditation process measures how well aligned one's program is with the mission statement.

In contrast, public schools are governed by superintendents and local school committees and are required to follow local, state, and federal guidelines and mandates. These regulations and restrictions usurp control from educators and often belittle the profession. In fact, the impositions and implications of the No Child Left Behind Act undermine all aspects of schooling—the curricular content, educational texts, the more scripted role of teachers, definitions of success, and the resulting rise in dropout rates.

Admissions is the first step in defining a school community. Private schools have their own admissions policies and screening processes in order to match student profiles with the school's beliefs and resources. It can be a highly competitive and often elitist process, including qualifying tests comparable to SATs scores for college. Since admissions policies vary greatly, admission can also be less formal and more inclusive. (At the Atrium, for instance, we have a lottery system of admissions.)

By contrast, a public school serves families and children within its district and can have an enormous range of needs to address. Rather than using the rigid methods and mandated testing dominant today, that range would be better served by offering various approaches and forms of assessment.

Some public and private schools share the challenge of providing a place where children can learn and grow in a diverse community. The costs of a private education can be prohibitive for many families, although many schools provide financial aid as generously as possible. For example, while the national average is about 8 percent of revenues, at the Atrium, the range is between 15 to 20 percent to allow for diversity. Public schools in urban and suburban areas have used busing and the models of magnet, pilot, and charter schools to create greater diversity than exists in a local neighborhood. Of course, the legacy of housing policies continues to affect the diversity of a neighborhood.

The size of the student population and the teacher–child ratio affect how supportive the school community is for faculty, parents, and students. Private schools have traditionally been on a smaller scale than their public counterparts with only a certain number of students admitted and a low student–teacher ratio. There has also been a recent "small schools" movement in public schools, led by Deborah Meier's Central Park East. Students and their capabilities, as well as their needs, are known in these schools. Yet, even now, the costly nature of small schools becomes a political issue, particularly for high schools.

Their different *financial structures* put different strains on public and private schools. Small private schools often are highly tuition dependent, so there is little financial security. The average salary of teachers is considerably less than that at public schools. In fact, some wonderful schools have had to close because of financial difficulties when their tuition base fluctuated even slightly. On the other hand, public schools, particularly urban and rural ones, have had their share of financial pulls and frustrations. Their funding is clearly linked to property taxes and the whims of cost-cutting officials and voters. There is a clear need to consider the notion of equity in funding. The state of Vermont has an innovative, progressive funding approach that can serve as a model for other states.

Perhaps the most important difference between public and private schools centers on the idea of freedom to *experiment*. Inherent in the word (as in Dewey's phrase "experimenting with the world") is the practice of bringing forth previous knowledge and experience and then observing, investigating, responding, and reflecting. This is true both for schools as institutions and teachers as individuals. Public schools, however, are subject to political scrutiny, dependent on political support, and used for political purposes. In fact, *experimenting* can be used as a dangerous word in public education ("Not on my children!"). Independent schools are autonomous entities and are free to develop innovative approaches.

The progressive tradition took root in independent schools. John Dewey, hero of many progressive educators, began the Laboratory School in 1896 with the express purpose of understanding how his theories worked in practice. A few years later, the Francis W. Parker School opened with a commitment to the intellectual, physical, and moral development of each individual student. Many other progressive schools have followed and their traditional counterparts have felt their influence. The notion of the child as active learner, the primacy of exploration and inquiry, the development of critical thinking skills, and the importance of collaborative learning—all emerge from the progressive tradition. Although they may be buzzwords even in traditional schools, they are at the heart of curriculum design in progressive ones.

Educators in independent private schools have both an opportunity and a responsibility to join the national forum on education. This means that private school faculties, administrators, and parents must stay informed about the implications of legislative choices and funding. These are clear first steps to be taken and sustained. Networking—at one's own workplace, attending conferences, joining organizations—and communicating with others (including parents, other educators, and politicians) are the means for building a powerful coalition.

We recognize and honor the complexities involved in reforming practices within all schools. And with this recognition, we acknowledge the energy and the determination needed to stay for the "long haul." Our hope, together as public and private school educators, is to parallel the collaborative work that we encourage in our students. Our responsibility is to articulate what is desirable, possible, and necessary.

PART THREE

Diversity and Antiracism

Head-on discussions of racism and equity run the risk of self-satisfied denial ("Not me! Not us!"); insensitivity; impersonality (arguments based on numbers); even, at times, a form of territoriality ("You don't belong, you can't know"). In the interest of showing rather than asserting, we include here four personal stories—stories with broad implications but with the advantages of authentic experience and individual voice.

Kathe Jervis tells the story of cultural misunderstanding between school and home, both of which were acting, according to their own assumptions and experience, in the best interests of the child—in this case one with special needs.

Joseph Suina, a Pueblo Indian, was educated in the American system which, at that time and in that place, was exemplified by the schoolteacher's command, "Leave your Indian [language] at home!" Suina describes the meaning of the loss of language and the dilemma felt by native populations trying to maintain their culture and identity in the face of the seductions of the "easy way of life of the whites."

Mara Sapon-Shevin recounts instances when expressions of racism and social prejudice in the classroom challenge both the "cool" and the resources of classroom teachers. As a teacher of teachers, Sapon-Shevin explores "teachable moments" that can transform potentially painful situations into opportunities for new understanding.

Louisa Cruz-Acosta brings sympathetic insights gained from her own growing up in New York as a "brown-skinned Puerto Rican girl" to dealing with a racial incident in her classroom. Again, the teacher (and the children) are caught between the values of the classroom-as-community and those of the surrounding society.

10

Is This Child Left Behind?

KATHE JERVIS

The story I'm about to tell draws attention to what happens when there is a clash of values between school and home. It raises the question: When significant differences arise, whose interests prevail, the family's or the school's? It highlights the difficult decisions that need to be made in this era of No Child Left Behind when teachers see children and their families reflected through their own cultural lenses.

At seven, Linda Zelaya's large sparkling brown eyes and warm open smile invite others to like her. Open, calm, trusting, eager to be engaged with a task, Linda likes school, but she loves swimming best. She loves museums and the museum-related art experiences both in and out of school. When a painting the class saw at the Brooklyn Museum showed up on a later trip to the Whitney Museum's Richard Diebenkorn retrospective, in the midst of the docent's talk to the sitting class, Linda stood up and uncharacteristically blurted out: "I know that painting!" as if she had encountered an old friend.

Linda loves the zoo ("You know, a museum where the animals move"). She invested herself in the tiniest details of her two pet crabs; they had names (Jack and Mary) and carefully observed habits. Jack died during the year and Linda saved Jack's quite beautiful shell to display in the room she shared with her sister. Linda relishes her relationship with her older sister, now in the classroom next door.

Linda, however, cannot read. As a researcher, I listened at intervals during Linda's second- and third-grade years to her attempts to decode her personal beloved copy of Dr. Seuss' *Green Eggs and Ham*. In the fall of third grade, she did not recognize the simplest words from one page to the next, including "the." Her supportive classroom teacher appreciated Linda's interests, kept copious anecdotal records, made numerous suggestions to the parents about free outside tutoring programs, and kept them informed of Linda's life at school. The teacher gained the Zelayas' trust because she recognized their dedicated support of their children. The parents gained the teacher's trust because their caring for their children was so visible. Outside Linda's classroom, however, other adults criticized. They thought Linda's inability to learn to read was her parents' fault.

Linda had a high absence rate of months at a time in kindergarten and first grade due to complications of moving from one geographical area to another. She was absent twenty-seven days in second grade, when she often stayed home to make extended family visits or just to keep her sister company when she was sick. Linda received help in the resource room. Early on during second grade, the resource room teacher said, "Linda is much slower than the others and I don't know whether to slow the rest down or let Linda float in the wind." This teacher blamed the parents: "Other parents help their kids for fifteen minutes a night. Why doesn't Linda's family?" When I myself first started observing Linda and her family as part of a federal study, I too had the hubris to believe that if Linda had lived in my reading and writing household, she would have made substantial progress.

In fact Linda lives with her parents and older sister in a tightly knit family. The Zelayas are strong parents, confident of their own beliefs and their children's strengths. Ms. Zelaya dropped out of school in tenth grade, and Mr. Zelaya is a high school graduate. After twenty years of driving a taxi and living on the economic margins, he is now a superintendent of an apartment building near the school. Their children's welfare is at the center of these parents' lives, and they did not see Linda as a child with deficits in need of remediation. Family life was central and they rejected any schedule or circumstance that interfered. Some families would have searched the city for a tutor to remediate Linda's reading difficulty. This family supported Linda as she was. Her parents never stopped believing that Linda would "learn in time."

But the school system, taking only academic progress into consideration, especially for those from outside the mainstream, did not bend to support these parents. When the special education team convened to report on their evaluation of Linda, each member of the team presented an expert portrait of Linda's deficits. The professional evidence in the report was clear; respect for the family and their perspective was not. Nowhere was the family's culture and devotion to their children acknowledged. And the genuine warmth the team felt for Linda (her "sunny smile and good nature") did not extend to her mother.

The team recommended Linda leave her current classroom for a special education class at another school— perhaps a reasonable solution from a professional point of view. Ms. Zelaya refused, saying calmly she needed to consult with her husband. Only an incomplete medical report on Linda's lazy eye kept the case open: Any unresolved medical condition that might explain a child's lack of progress is grounds for delaying a special education assignment. Otherwise Ms. Zelaya would have had to submit to an immediate district-level arbitration that very day in order to appeal the school-based team's decision. She would then have had to abide by that decision or lose all remedial services for her daughter. (Ironically, these policies were developed to protect the rights of families and children, even as they increased the adversarial nature of home–school relationships.)

After this evaluation meeting, I went back home with Ms. Zelaya. She said about the recommendation: "I will never put my child on a yellow bus to attend a different school away from her sister. No way! I'll take her out of school before I do that." Only when I had my coat on to leave did she admit how upset and demeaned she felt without her husband at the meeting: "He is older, he understands more. I don't know how to talk in meetings like this. I was afraid I would sound ignorant. Did I sound stupid?" she wanted to know. The deficit labels applied to Linda had washed over her; she was more troubled by feeling outclassed by experts with whom she had no relationship. Had her husband been with her, it would have made all the difference in the meeting for her feelings, but it would not have affected her absolute refusal to send Linda to another school. A few days later, Ms. Zelaya said, "It took me until I took a shower that night to cry about how the meeting made me feel."

Ms. Zelaya's experience is not necessarily a matter of ethnicity. When my five-year-old daughter had a test to measure her brain waves, the well-meaning pediatric neurologist kindly read the results immediately right in front of us: "She has an abnormal brain and clumsy child syndrome." I couldn't think of a single question or comment. It took three days before my daughter asked me what *clumsy* meant. I was in the same situation as Ms. Zelaya and I wished my husband had been there too. Unless experts create space for questioning, and convey willingness to take time to answer, the appearance of mute compliance will continue to be the norm—especially when the topic under discussion is anxiety-provoking.

Linda's lazy eye saved her for that year and she was socially promoted to fourth grade. At the beginning of that year, it was immediately clear that Linda could not keep up in the classroom, which was organized very differently from her third-grade class. By now Mr. and Ms. Zelaya were ready to let Linda go to another school; her sister had graduated and gone to the local Catholic school. Linda, a year older, was by this time ready to leave a classroom where every day it was clear she could not keep up with the volume of seatwork. The school and district-level evaluators recommended a small class in a neighboring school, which happily had an opening for Linda. The teacher had once taught at Linda's previous school.

When I visited Linda's new teacher, she expressed in one breath two contradictory opinions, which go to the heart of the matter: "Linda has more general knowledge than any other child in the class. You can tell kids who have been in special ed for a long time because their curriculum has been so narrowly focused on skills;" and "Why didn't her teacher send Linda to special ed earlier? Shame on her."

Linda's former second/third grade teacher does not consider this a poor decision—there was no choice: "These strong parents knew their kid and refused all other choices." The parents may have been intimidated by the school "experts" who tried to tell them what to do, but they refused to bend to anything that did not support their family values.

Linda and her parents were much readier the next year for this change, and after three months in the fourth-grade special education class, Linda could sail through *Green Eggs and Ham*. Her progress perhaps was due to method (an intensive focus on memorizing a list of sight words), to her greater age, or to other unknowable circumstances. Chapter books are still some time away, but Linda and her parents fully expect her to get there on her own schedule. However, she will fail by an external standard: She cannot pass a standardized test required by the George W. Bush No Child Left Behind Act.

This story can be read as failure—an unbridgeable cultural gap between home and school resulting in irreconcilable differences. Or, it can be read as a success—a caring teacher resisting conventional school solutions and joining in a family's willingness to wait, protecting a family's values even at the expense of the child's formal academic progress. Linda's family's interpretation of the world was different from that of the school, which still raises the question: If the school's main responsibility is to equip children with skills needed for further education, what should the school do when that aim is frustrated by a child's low achievement and a family's willingness to wait until the child is ready? This is a dilemma for all schools when external demands squeeze children and their families too tightly in a standardized vise.

Trust between schools and families is not a given. Trust is the expectation that someone in a position to do harm will do no harm. The Zelayas felt that professionals who ignored their values could very well do them harm, even if it was not what the adults in the school intended. The solution is some form of reciprocal relationship that will foster a degree of empathy and understanding of each other's perspectives. Educators, for their part, must move beyond the stereotype that parents outside the middle-class mainstream "don't care" about their children's education when they make choices different from those made by the school.

Guadalupe Valdez (1996) has pointed out—with sadness—that a school's ability to educate is judged against a mainstream culture of achievement with its focus on individual upward mobility rather than an understanding of home values. This description of Linda and her family dramatizes the wisdom of that statement.

11

Tongue-Tied Again
Policy, Schooling, and American Indian Tribes

JOSEPH SUINA

ederal government policies ostensibly designed to promote the integration of American Indians into the outside world have almost always yielded negative results. Practice rarely meets intention. Recently, the federal policy No Child Left Behind has placed programs and even personnel in a precarious situation in the schools where there have been promising gains for cultural and language inclusion. In some ways it has been like a step back in time to the days when native culture and language use in the classroom were strictly forbidden.

It has taken many years to make the inclusion of the native culture and language in the schools possible and now they are once again threatened by the zealous return to the tight, white-knuckled Eurocentric grip of control on what is sanctioned in the classroom. In the name of accountability, with testing as the whipping post, there is a return to a greater degree of the old-fashioned Indian schooling and its classroom values: nothing less than total assimilation in respect to knowledge, skills, and attitudes to succeed in the American economy. It is difficult for tribes to argue against accountability, good test scores, and good jobs for their children, but there are clear negative ramifications for American Indian and other minority cultures in the United States. The message is loud and clear: Native culture and language "had better take a back seat in the bus" or you won't pass the test.

The first day of school for me was one talked about with a great deal of apprehension and fear, after all it was a completely different world that my five- and six-year-old Pueblo peers and I were about to enter. Our parents reassured and even coached us in how to respond to what was sure to come that very first school day, as this was the same white teacher who received them at our age a generation before. My uncle did a terrific imitation of her to make us laugh and diffuse some of the tension that had built up in me. The first day came and sure enough the words—"What is your name little boy?"—came forth in her raspy "cigarette voice" just as expected. Some of us nonspeakers were prepared to meet this challenge. Anthony was not. He turned around to us, puzzled, looking for any clue with which we might support him. We offered him cautious whispers in our native Keres language, "E shra nee" (your name). In turn, Anthony queried, "Ah asha nee?" (my name?), at which the teacher quickly responded, "Oh, Anthony, what a nice name!" She took the approximation for the correct answer; clearly, she was not yet frustrated with our ignorance.

Among the first English words we learned in school were, "Leave your Indian at home!" because they were spoken often and with disdain. This command, the trademark of the school, was announced loudly and clearly within the school grounds. A prominent barbwire fence to keep out both the cows and our native tongue completely insulated the school. The teacher was resolute and once we passed that school fence into her world any utterance of the forbidden language brought on her wrath. We were poignantly reminded of the consequences of a relapse into our former selves by a nearby ruler to rap our hands and a handy piece of soap for our mouths. Before too long I became acquainted with the sharp and putrid taste of lye that would hang bitter for some time after treatment.

Taking away our home language was like having our very breath of life cut off. It was most difficult to go expressionless, to lose the words that gave meaning to our young lives and to lose all references with which to make sense of this new and bewildering world before us. Our easygoing verbal bantering and laughter was suffocated by the authoritarian demand for obedience and use of English only. It was as if our social lubricant was literally being dried up within us in those early days of school. Fortunately for us, the joy of voice returned quickly as soon as we stepped on the other side of the line of demarcation—the barbwire fence. Our spirits rekindled and shouts in Keres and laughter rang out across the late afternoon air within earshot of the teacher's home. Although we never spoke about our immediate actions beyond the school grounds, we knew this was freedom and I think secretly we all wanted our oppressor to know we were not stripped of ourselves.

Our parents and the tribal leadership never complained about the school's blatant attack on our language. Perhaps because they knew nothing would be done about it anyway; this was and is still, for the most part, the norm when Indians deal with Bureau of Indian Affairs. And having been through this experience themselves, they probably figured school was just that way; a bitter pill for some future well-being. After all, they wanted better opportunities in life for us, and for all the pain, English was an important tool. It was difficult for our tribe to argue against the promise of a better future for us even then. More important, I think our elders just assumed that our language would continue no matter what, as it had since time immemorial.

There was the school and there was the Pueblo and the two rarely met except when villagers came to watch us perform in the school Christmas play once a year. Each side of the fence had its own focus, and it seemed it was better not to get in each other's way. As children, we were the ones caught up in both cultures and were affected deeply by each whether the adults wanted to recognize it or not.

Background

My Pueblo is among the nineteen separate and sovereign nations in New Mexico, the Hopi nation with twelve villages in Arizona and the nation of Yesleta Pueblo in El Paso, Texas. They make up today's Pueblo Indians of the Southwest, the descendants of the Anasazi—the cliff dwellers of prehistoric times. Each tribe is autonomous and unique with its own government and cultural infrastructure. Yet the similarities across groups are easy to spot. While every one of the Pueblos has retained a good measure of its cultural heritage, often recognized as the least culturally changed among the U.S. indigenous groups, all have been experiencing language shift for many years. For many, this shift has advanced to a crisis stage where only the grandparent generation is truly fluent in the native language.

Anxiety over the state of the native tongue has led to efforts by several Pueblos to stem further erosion by implementing alternative language teaching formats in a variety of settings. The move toward more nuclear single-family dwellings, thanks to still another government initiative, HUD (U.S. Housing and Urban Development) housing on the reservation, unlike the traditional living patterns, has caused the majority of young Pueblo families to be without a native speaker in the home. For this and other reasons, language revitalization in the most natural settings, home and village, has met with limited success. In spite of the elders' frequent encouragement to use the language, revitalization of the language is much more difficult than anyone anticipated. Television, the Internet, and other modern devices are tough competition for the native language revival for youth and their parents. Ironically, schools have thus become an important venue for native language revival.

In school, students are a captive audience in one location and present on a regular basis. Because of the important potential of this setting, the Pueblos have attempted to carve out a place in school in ways they have never done before. Although native language and culture are not on equal footing with other school subjects, significant gains have been made to include them where once they were strictly forbidden. Pueblo elders come to school from the villages to teach the language and use traditional knowledge and wisdom as curriculum material to achieve this in forty-five-minute periods throughout the day. These native language teachers, however, are the first to recognize that schools cannot do it alone.

There have also been attempts to provide after-school language classes for parents who are non-native speakers but parents are difficult to gather in one location after a long work day. Are parents motivated enough to go all out to recapture the language and preserve the culture? The answer can only come with time. A religious leader in our ceremonial chamber, the kiva, predicted that it would not be the church, the government, or even the schools that would cause the downfall of our culture; the cause would be our indifference toward our own culture and our fascination and preoccupation with the seemingly easy way of life of the whites.

History of Indian Schooling

The government policy of total assimilation of Indian youth in the late 1800s and early 1900s was intended for Indians to eventually melt into the white culture. Children were the catalyst in this process and many, as young as six, were removed from their homes and villages to distant boarding schools—some more than a thousand miles away. The purpose was to extract them from the "contamination" of their native culture and to make clear the way for the inevitable complete cultural transformation. A child who left at age six might not have been seen again on the reservation until in his or her late teens or early twenties. During the summer, the child was sent to live with a white farmer, a blacksmith, or a carpenter in a program the government referred to as the "Outing System." It was designed "to drench" the Indian youth completely in the ways of the white man. The long-term goal was to return to the tribes transformed young adults who would in turn change their tribes with their newly acquired knowledge, skills, and attitudes. Funded by the U.S. Congress, the first among the many boarding schools that sprang up in the next fifty years was the infamous Carlisle Indian School in Pennsylvania in 1887. It was America's way of dealing with the so-called "Indian problem" soon after the Civil War. Many children never came home. They died in those schools, some say just from loneliness. Today, grave markers of all the Indian children who died as the result of a government policy can be viewed at the old site of the Carlisle Indian School.

This policy, as with most other "wonderful" government ideas on behalf of Indian tribes, failed miserably. Returned youth were unsuccessful in fulfilling the *great white father's* plan to make changes from within and instead they became misfits and even outcasts in their own communities. Many moved out to nearby towns never to be heard from again. American public outcry against this inhumane treatment of the Indians finally rose to a high crescendo. The 1928 Meriam Report was the most comprehensive account of U.S.–Indian relations, and it gave Indian boarding schools the most scathing reviews of all. As a result, Indian schools were brought closer to the reservations but the effort to destroy the native culture and language remained relentless and vital into the mid-1950s right in the backyards of Pueblo villages as the preceding accounts illustrate.

Importance of the Native Language

In the Pueblos the native language is paramount in maintaining all aspects of traditional life. The culture is oral. Written language has never been allowed in most Pueblos because of the function the living language serves as the social and religious connection between the generations. It is the glue that binds all dimensions of our existence together in the Pueblo culture; our relationships with each other and with all of nature are defined by the words we speak in this life and the hereafter. One elder questioned, "How do we pray to our ancestral spirits if they don't understand English?" He meant more than just mere understanding of the words.

The erosion of the native language is potentially the gravest threat faced by the Pueblos. Without the language the theocratic form of government through which laypeople assume responsibility for service to the people will crumble and the Pueblos' interdependent life values, which define what it is to be a tribal member, will be shaken to the core. This perception is shared by many Pueblos who now wonder, however, whether the effort to revive the language is already too little too late.

Formal schooling as promoted by the outside government policy over the last one hundred years could not have been more at odds with the needs of the Pueblos. The seeds of early practices in Indian schooling have finally sprouted and taken root. Still in this day of so-called multicultural literacy, we hear teachers argue that it is not their duty to promote the culture and the language of the Indians; that their job is to prepare students for the world of work. Their work is simplified by focusing on the subject matter and not on the children. Some tribes agree with this approach. It does, however, disregard the damaging effects of an education that is totally focused on passing tests for better job opportunities in the future. Indian tribes and the poor in America are particularly susceptible to this stunted view of education since they worry more about the immediate needs in their lives, like jobs. Education is not seen within the framework of educating children for a democratic society. Children need to know more than just how to read; they need to know "how to read between the lines" if they are to bring about social justice in schools and in society.

As indicated before, due to tribal insistence it is the school—the very instrument that did so much to harm the health of native languages—that is looked to now to revive the language. Will the new policies once again do harm to Indian people?

Today, with many Pueblo languages in a critical state of deterioration, an often-pondered question is: Will the culture survive without the language? Many think not, thus all the attention paid to this particular area of culture in each of our Pueblos. Is it possible that the culture, which has sustained our people through all the trials and tribulations brought on by three outside governments since the coming of the Europeans, will soon come to an end? Elders tell us of our people having survived before the European invasion, for hundreds and perhaps thousands of years in the face of challenges from other pillaging tribes and the natural elements, thanks to our culture. How do we tell our children and how do we answer to our ancestors that we have abandoned what was entrusted in us to continue?

12

Teachable Moments for Social Justice

MARA SAPON-SHEVIN

A teacher approaches me in tears: There have been repeated racial incidents on her school's playground and she feels an urgent need to engage students in discussion and action related to creating safe schools and accepting communities. But when she brings this imperative to the school administrators, she is reminded that the statewide standardized tests are coming up soon and there simply isn't time to address these issues with students. The teacher is told that she must concentrate exclusively on academic achievement so that the school will look good on the tests and not risk funding cuts or negative publicity. Her attempts to explain the relationship between students' sense of safety and belonging and achievement scores are dismissed as interesting but not compelling.

The diversity of students in today's schools and the ways in which poverty, racism, and violence creep—and sometimes stomp—into our classrooms present a host of challenges for teachers. How do we create classroom climates that embody equity, social justice, inclusion, and diversity while still achieving high "academic" standards? If the pressures of multiple agendas were not enough to leave us depleted and overwhelmed, the growing focus (one might say manic emphasis) on high-stakes standardized testing has left many progressive educators even more frustrated. How do we maintain our focus on democratic, child-centered education in the face of a system that tells us that test scores are all that matters, and that there isn't enough time to pursue what are often labeled "soft" or secondary educational goals such as classroom community or a commitment to ending racism and other oppressions?

Acknowledgment: Much appreciation to Christin Hogan, Courtney Mosher, Cynthia Johnson, and Jeanette Decker for their contribution of teachable moments.

To some, making a commitment to social justice means that we must add a whole new "program" to an already overcrowded curriculum. In reality, however, there are "teachable moments" for social justice *everywhere* and a teacher who is primed and committed to noticing and responding to such moments can infuse values about belonging, right treatment, and justice throughout the day. Consider, for example, what teaching opportunities are provided by the following situations:

- A fifth-grade boy draws swastikas on the paper of the only Jewish girl in the class.
- As they do their seatwork, students are pulling up the sides of their eyes to look "Asian" and chanting a rhyme about Japanese and Chinese people.
- A ninth grader is slammed against the locker in the hallway and told he is a "stupid little faggot" and he better watch where he walks.
- As a teacher constructs her birthday chart and discusses how they will celebrate birthdays in her class, a young boy raises his hand and explains that he's not allowed to celebrate birthdays and another girl says that she heard that people from Africa sometimes don't know when their birthdays are and wonders how they celebrate.

All of these are real incidents, and no doubt teachers can think of many more within their own classrooms and schools. The challenge is to respond in productive, educative ways that help all of us move toward a more inclusive and diverse society rather than letting them go by, either because we don't notice them or because we feel inadequate to respond or too rushed to prioritize such efforts. I have categorized teachable moments for social justice into two groups: *seized* and *lost*. For the last five years, I have asked my preservice teacher education students to document teachable moments for social justice that they have seen in their classrooms, heightening their awareness of both good teaching and encouraging them to observe the conditions of schools and classrooms that make responding productively more or less likely.

Being able to respond requires both noticing that the moment "happened" and having some response ready. For example, after the September 11, 2001, attacks on the World Trade Center in New York City, a boy in one teacher's fifth-grade class announced, "I think all Muslims should be sent back to their countries because they're all terrorists." The teacher, rather than criticizing the boy, engaged the class in a discussion. "Hmmm," she said, "I wonder how many of you remember the Oklahoma City bombing?" Many of the students raised their hands. "And who did it turn out was responsible for that?" she asked. "Timothy McVeigh," the students responded. "And what religion was he?" she persisted. "Catholic," they answered. "And how many of you are Catholic?" she asked, knowing the demographics already. Many hands went up. "Then I wonder if we should send all the Catholics in our class away because they might be dangerous terrorists." The students were shocked and protested, "Of course not, that was about him, not about being Catholic, that's not what they teach us at church," and on and on.

This teacher was able to challenge the dangerously problematic statement of a student by converting it to a powerful teachable moment about prejudice, stereotyping, and overgeneralization. Such lessons are precious and need to be actively encouraged. We all need better repertoires for responding to oppressive behavior and language.

Sometimes our responses are inadequate because although we *noticed* the moment, we are unsure about how to respond. In one first-grade classroom, students were drawing at their tables. One student looked over at another and said derisively, "You're Puerto Rican." The teacher, alert to the negative tone in the statement, responded quickly. "Don't say that!" and ended the conversation. Although she was, no doubt, responding to the pejorative tone with which the girl's ethnicity was mentioned, I worry that the message the students got was, "Don't talk about it"—don't notice or discuss people's differences in skin color, language, or ethnicity. What would have had to be in place for the teacher to make another response? Perhaps to ask the "name calling" girl what she knows about Puerto Rico, or how she knows someone is Puerto Rican. Maybe the girl singled out, who was in fact Puerto Rican, might have been asked to share something of her own story at an appropriate moment.

Our ability to respond constructively when teachable moments come up is not a simple matter. First, we must improve our sensitivity to the occurrence of the teaching occasion, our ability to "notice." This requires a store of relevant information. We must know enough about Islam to be alert to other students' remarks about "starving" during Ramadan, or to students' confusion between religion, ethnicity, skin color, and citizenship.

Similarly, it will be difficult to respond to the student who says that gay people caused AIDS if we don't know anything about the history of the disease or the ways in which it's spread. Simply put, we must learn more about different groups, about the ways in which oppression manifests itself, and about the occasions that might be problematic or give rise to teasing, exclusion, or mistreatment. Reading widely, talking to those outside our own group, pushing our own comfort level, asking respectful questions, all these can help us to get smarter about oppression. Maintaining an attitude of alertness is also critical: What are students saying to one another during work time? Who has no one to sit with at lunch? What was the fight on the playground about and how was it resolved? Although it is painful to notice things we feel powerless to change, *not* noticing gives students the message that oppression is inevitable and countering mistreatments is hopeless. Even if we can do no more than notice and name the oppression, we model for students the powerful message that injustice is not invisible or acceptable.

Second, we must have structures and policies in place in our classrooms that make productive responses possible. After September 11, 2001, for example, teachers who had already established a strong classroom community found themselves better able to respond to the devastating tragedy and all the feelings and responses it provoked. Teachers who already had established a morning meeting and guidelines for community discussion, those who had their students keep journals, and schools that had a strong school–parent relationship were able to rally and respond more quickly.

One elementary teacher who already had a word wall, which included the words *prejudice, discrimination,* and *acceptance,* was able to refer to those words when discussing the targeting of Arabs in the community and the importance of learning about others before jumping to conclusions. In classrooms that begin with an individual check-in for each student, teachers are more likely to be able to take the temperature of their classes' social climate and have ways to respond.

Third, teachers need to develop repertoires for responding to social justice moments. Some of these responses are invariably reactive—we don't know that something will happen until it does. But sometimes sensitive teachers can predict that various experiences or processes will demand social justice teaching and do so proactively. For example, when one teacher's class was about to visit a home for older adults to interact with the residents, she engaged them in lengthy lessons on how to introduce themselves, how people's abilities to speak and hear may be impaired with age, and how to respond respectfully and thoughtfully, and what it means to treat *all* people with dignity. The teacher's ability to prevent certain kinds of negative behavior was a function of her careful preparation of her students for the experience they were about to have.

Teachers whose classrooms include students with a wide range of skills and abilities have unique opportunities to teach about individual differences, how and when to help one another, and what it means to be a community. This kind of preparation is far preferable to saying nothing and then needing to respond to comments such as "You're stupid 'cause you read baby books" or "People who drool are disgusting!"

When our responses are commonly reactive, we need to know other ways that are age-appropriate and educative rather than punitive. The teacher responding to the statement about expelling all the Muslims was able to connect her students to their own experience in a way that was immediately transparent to them. When students in a second-grade class started laughing about a story in which a child's letter to her grandma ended with X's and O's (symbolizing hugs and kisses), the teacher was able to connect their discomfort to experiences in their own lives in which affection or physical contact was somehow constrained or ridiculed. The teacher was able to lead them in a discussion of all the ways in which people show one another they love each other, as well as to point out differences between families, cultures, and situations.

Finally, we must continually renew our personal commitment to counteracting racism, homophobia, classism, and other forms of oppression and work hard to encourage one another—that is, to give one another courage—to act decisively even when we feel inadequate to the task. The struggle to create and nurture democratic, inclusive schools and classrooms requires great fortitude and resilience.

Many current educational initiatives are directly incompatible with fostering children's individual differences and the formation of cohesive, supportive learning communities. We need to share our successes and our failures in working for social justice with one another and to learn how to support each other as we work to create schools and communities of justice and peace.

13

Friendship and Social Justice in a Kindergarten Classroom

LOUISA CRUZ-ACOSTA

O ne spring morning in 1995, Darwin rushed up to me in the middle of "Work/Choice Time," eyes wide with astonishment, and blurted out: "Louisa! you gotta hear what Nuyen just told me! Nuyen's mommy said she can't be my friend anymore because I am black and she says black people are bad!"

Standing next to him, Nuyen seemed resigned to this new reality. She hung her head in silence. Yet, there she was, by his side as always. Suddenly, I was confronted with one of those moments every teacher dreads: a difficult, complicated situation that just pops up out of nowhere. For the first few moments, I felt completely unprepared—confused and powerless.

As a brown-skinned Puerto Rican girl living in New York City, I grew up aware of the painful realities of life in a racialized world. In the public schools I attended, I'd been witness to countless subtle and not so subtle distinctions made between white children and children of color; distinctions made by teachers, by principals, even by my own family. Time and again, I observed children with light skin treated as though they deserved more care and attention than children with dark skin. Experiencing the same phenomenon again at that moment in my teaching career was difficult. The possibility that a parent could threaten the values I held for my classroom—a sense of community and inclusion among the children—gave me grave concern. I have always believed children need a strong sense of community; that it is an

My deepest gratitude to Elaine Avidon, teacher, mentor, friend, without whom this and other teaching stories would never have made it to the printed page.

essential factor in their ability to thrive as learners and understand their relationship to other human beings.

In *Teacher with a Heart* (1998a), Vito Perrone, former dean at the University of North Dakota and Harvard's Graduate School of Education, narrates stories of his own and the teaching life of Leonard Covello, a New York City high school principal in the East Harlem of the 1950s. He describes the principle and students joining together to form a community:

> I am now more conscious of Covello's single-mindedness about the importance of community, that sense of collective caring, of solidarity. These are particularly important matters for contemporary schools, struggling as they are with the diversity of their students and related communities, trying desperately to build among their students solid commitments to powerful learning. (1998a, 4)

On that morning, forty years after Covello lived and worked in a similar community, two young children stood before me, presenting an issue I was not sure I was prepared to handle.

Nuyen, a five-year-old Vietnamese girl, had recently moved to New York with her family. Barely able to communicate with anyone except her parents and an older brother, she was now friendly with this boy she'd met only a short time ago.

Darwin had experienced some difficulty adjusting to school, therefore his relationship with his kindergarten teacher was somewhat strained and tense. I'd offered our class as an alternative place to be until he and his teacher could work things out. When he first joined the class, I introduced him as "our guest" and explained that he would be with us for a while. I shared some of my childhood experiences with my students; talked about how my family was larger than just the people who lived with me; how we were often visited for long periods of time by aunts, uncles, and cousins who came from Puerto Rico and other parts of the city. I described the situation as a special time filled with opportunities for learning and having great fun. While Darwin was calm and pleasant to me during those first visits, he showed no interest in the children or in becoming part of the class. Most days, he just sat drawing at a table in silence.

Morning Meeting was a special time for the class: A time when the children and I sat together on a large rug to talk, play, and read one of the picture books from our class library. We prepared for the day by talking about the weather, how we'd traveled to school, and discussed what the day ahead looked like. As we discussed the children's choice of activity each morning and who they wished to play with, Nuyen sat silently on the rug and watched Darwin draw. Once Morning Meeting ended, the children rose from their spots and went to work.

Each day Darwin sat at the same table, drawing without speaking to anyone. At first, if a child went near him, tried to talk to him, or asked questions about his work, he glared at them and growled, "Leave me alone!" They respected his request. This went on for a few days. I don't quite remember when the two children noticed each other or who made the first overture. I imagine, however, that it was Nuyen. I vaguely remember her quietly inviting him to build with her in the block area. I can still see them moving about rapidly; him, planning what they would make, choosing what blocks and accessories they would need. He spoke to her and interacted in ways his teacher and I had never witnessed, with animation and excitement. He found pictures of buildings I'd clipped from magazines and showed them to Nuyen as samples of structures they could build. She smiled a lot and followed his lead, saying very little, letting her actions speak for her. I began to notice that in the course of their developing friendship, Nuyen's ability to communicate in English grew. Darwin's self-confidence grew too; he became interested in other children in the class and was eventually able to make more friends.

One day, then, completely unexpectedly, Darwin and Nuyen were standing before me announcing that their friendship had to end. As they stared up at me, I felt stunned, thinking, "What am I supposed to say? What is the 'appropriate' reaction? Do they understand what they have just asked of me?" Yet, I now believe that, in a very profound way, they did. They wanted only to continue their friendship, to enjoy inventing stories, building with blocks, planning what they would play at recess. I was the teacher, the adult. They knew it was my job to make that possible. I realized there would be no easy solution. I asked what they thought we could do as I tried to catch my breath while my mind raced.

The strategy I most rely on in moments of conflict between children is giving them time to sort through the matter themselves while mediating for them as they express their feelings. When they cannot speak to each other calmly, I ask that they draw and write about the problem and later share their work with each other. This serves as a way of helping them to communicate about difficult feelings.

I asked the two children whether they thought we could write a letter to Nuyen's mother, whether they thought that it might help. Familiar with this strategy from past experience, they both agreed it was worth a try. Then, I specifically asked Nuyen if *she* thought it might work. I knew she was struggling to find a way to be heard without appearing to rebel against her mother's authority. I was very familiar with this dilemma, having grown up in a similar world that believed adults had the only real authority. To my surprise, Nuyen was enthusiastic and agreed to deliver the letter.

I sat outside our classroom with the children, while the other children remained busy with their projects, just a few feet away. With Darwin sitting on one side of me and Nuyen on the other, I folded a large sheet of unlined paper, the kind Darwin used every day, and asked that they begin. As they drew, I sat between them, watching. Darwin drew a picture of himself in his bright red Chicago Bulls jersey and blue jeans and Nuyen drew the same picture and added one of herself standing next to him. I then asked: "What words should we write?" Darwin was quick to answer:

Dear Nuyen's mom:

I like you. You are nice. I want to be Nuyen's friend
because we have fun.

Just then, Nuyen added:

I want to still be Darwin's friend. He teaches me lots
of things and we have fun. He is not bad.

They then signed the letter; it went home with Nuyen that day.

Days passed. The children's friendship continued. They played together every day, building and writing; inventing stories to go with the complex structures they created in the block area; playing Darwin's favorite sport, football, at recess. Weeks passed. I did not ask what had happened for fear I would have to then figure out some way to keep the children apart. "No news was good news" I thought, and we just went on with our lives.

One afternoon, Darwin mentioned that he and Nuyen had been on a play date. When I asked about it, Darwin cheerfully explained that their mothers had met at the bus stop and Nuyen's mom had apologized to Darwin and to his mom. After that initial encounter, the children were allowed frequent play dates in each other's homes.

This story illustrates how important children's own words can be, how instructive and powerful an experience it is when they are truly heard and supported in finding a solution to a problem they might not have been able to solve on their own. As Patricia Carini states in "Building from Children's Strengths": "All children seek to make sense of their world and hold in common a questioning, wondering posture" (1986, 17).

In many ways I'd felt as vulnerable as the children that day. I was suddenly involved in an uncomfortable conflict between people of different races. In an effort to be a good parent and to protect her daughter, Nuyen's mother had accepted a damaging stereotype and was forcing her child to agree with this prejudiced view of Darwin and "his kind of people."

However, by seeking help and acting on their feelings, Darwin and Nuyen had helped the adults see past strong personal biases.

As their teacher, I had been so grateful that Nuyen and Darwin had found each other to rely on and to encourage each other. It had been a saving grace. I was also in awe of their ability to take that risk, to take a chance on friendship. Their actions had a profound effect on me.

My own history, the experiences I'd had in schools where children were compared and contrasted based on their performance and on racial and social stratifications, created in me a strong sense of the importance of inclusion. I wholeheartedly agreed that "[w]e need to find ways of supporting students to move beyond their physical and cultural boundaries, to meet, work with and get to know others better" (Perrone 1998a, 20). Yet, one parent's beliefs and the demands she placed on her child were in direct conflict with the values I held and tried to model for my young students.

It might seem that the matter of who a child could play with, be friends with, would not be in the realm of a teacher's control, that a parent's decision about such matters should prevail. Yet, because it had such direct and serious repercussions on the life of our classroom community, I felt obligated to respond—to make a strong and clear statement to the children. If indeed I believed that part of my responsibility as a teacher was to serve as an agent of social change, it was clear I would have to act in accordance with those principles.

Reflecting on the situation as I have so many times since then, I have come to realize what an incredible opportunity I was given on that day. Just one moment in my personal and professional development, that situation forced me to truly examine my beliefs in a real situation, to put to them to the test when it most mattered: when it had the potential to influence my students in a substantial way.

This experience, though difficult, also provided a vital opportunity for the children. It had created the ground in which their sense of social responsibility could begin to take root. In the end, it proved to be an important opportunity for us all to recognize children's ability to work out solutions to difficult situations when their own interests (like friendships) are at stake. These two children were helped to find a solution that enabled them to keep playing together, to continue being friends, and to learn from each other. It also validated my beliefs in the foundation of our classroom community: racial equality and social justice. Friendship, equality, and justice—yes, these were very high stakes indeed.

PART FOUR

Children and the Curriculum

Amidst all the talk in educational policy circles about corporate needs, "scientific" methods, standards, and marketable skills, the simple phrase from the Plowden Report (quoted earlier) again comes to mind: "At the heart of the educational process lies the child." The chapters in this part focus on the child and, in one context or another, on intrinsic interest as motivation for learning (as opposed to test-driven motivation).

Anne Martin reminds us that writing for young children is a means of extending "thinking, feeling, and speaking," not just a matter of teaching skills. Hubert and Rebecca Dyasi link four "frameworks" for progressive education, from their experiences growing up and becoming professionals in Africa, then later in New York at the Workshop Center (CCNY) and also in the NDSG. Brenda Engel describes one young child's own standards for her artwork with implications for sources of standards in all creative work.

Finally, Deborah Meier describes the current climate of academic pressures on children, along with the loss of the company of adults. Meier specifies the risks of no longer allowing time, or making accommodation, for children's natural ways of learning—through imitation, exploration, and invention.

14

From Mind to Hand

Beginning Writers

ANNE MARTIN

once upon a time ther was a bird and she loved to sing but her hasband did not like it but one day they saw a singing movie on tv then they saing to gather.

—KARIN, AGE 5

Not so long ago, before the advent of movements like "Process Writing" and "Whole Language," young children were not expected to write stories independently, even before they had learned to read. When I started teaching kindergarten in a New York City public school in the early 1960s, I was chastised by a supervisor for displaying written text around the room on charts, on the blackboard, on walls. In those days it was considered sacrilegious to expose young children to print or to teach letters and sounds that might stimulate interest in reading and writing. The children were supposed to use only concrete play materials and learn from their own discoveries without being pressured to acquire academic skills too early. I was praised for my emphasis on blocks, paints, puzzles, music, stories, drama, but discouraged from including literacy activities as well.

Those days must seem unbelievable now when the whole thrust of kindergarten programs has gone in the opposite direction, where most of the day is spent on drill work in phonics (much of it through worksheets that require neatness and coloring within the lines), handwriting, spelling, and number concepts. Today teachers are usually told what and how to teach, and presented with mandated detailed curricula to be used in every area of study, complete with scripted lessons to deliver to their classes.

In those standardized reading and writing lessons, young children are no more given the freedom to experiment with their own ways of learning to read and write than they were in the time when literacy was considered out of bounds. Children as young as four years old are given sheets with words to copy repeatedly in block letters on lined paper, and their one-word papers (e.g., APPLE or SNOW) are hung up in the halls for parents to admire. Sometimes the children don't know what they have copied, sometimes their coordination is not up to the task, and sometimes they dislike these exercises, but in many classrooms this is the method used to teach writing to beginners, as early as possible.

However, children generally do not need to be coerced to learn to write. Ask a kindergarten child on the first day of school to write something, and for every child who looks blank and says, "But I don't know how to write," there are many others who will settle right down to draw, often telling a story to go with the picture. "Look," said Lora, "I writed a girl and a umbrella and colored rain." Drawing and writing are so closely allied for young children that one can arise from the other. Indeed, many children talk to themselves steadily as they draw, telling the story of what is taking form on their papers, and others may draw silently but have a great deal to say when they have finished their pictures. While telling is not writing, having things to say is what can motivate children to tackle the formidable technical difficulties of writing: physical control of a writing tool, sounds of letters, shapes and sizes of letters, the order of letters in a word and sentence, spelling (often irrational), the concentration to put all these together and make some sense. It's a wonder that so many five- and six-year-olds are able to make a start at all.

Of course, "writing" doesn't necessarily mean stories and poems to a young child. It might just mean filling pages with letters, numbers, names, or words copied from signs, books, or TV. I saw my task in teaching writing to kindergarten children as the attempt to make clear the connection between the children's pleasure in manipulating language orally and their pleasure in doodling on a piece of paper. Out of everyday storytelling, listening to books, engaging in the arts and working with math and science materials, writing emerges as a new and different dimension that expands a child's possibilities for expression.

Lora, who "writed" her pictures at the beginning of the year, was writing stories by springtime. Like many beginning writers, she found a way to separate her words by using dashes between them, rather than trusting in blank spaces:

WIN-DAY-I-LT-MY-BRD-GO-AT FLAD-A-WAY-THE-NAKST-DAY-I-GAT-A-NW-BRD-AND-I-LOVE-MY -NW-BRD-I-LT-MY-BRD-GO-BY-KS I-WS-GT-EG-A-NE-PAPE-THE-END

[One day I let my bird go. It flied away. The next day I got a new bird and I love my new bird. I let my bird go because I was getting a new puppy. The End.]

It is evident that Lora had already learned a great deal about writing. She knew that words are separated; she spelled many words correctly and the others phonetically enough for someone else to read; although she didn't know the "ing" spelling, she approximated with "eg." Most of all, she had some sense of story form and her responsibility to a reader, starting off with "One day," marking "The end," and explaining her actions in the story.

The subject matter of children's writing often derives directly from classroom activities. Natural science, which was always a large part of my curriculum, provided opportunities and material for children's writing, sparked by the many group observations, which I recorded for the class on chart paper. The children got so used to my writing things down that they sometimes held me to it even when I thought we were just chatting informally. "Write it down! Write it down!" one little girl kept insisting, until she was satisfied that I was keeping notes.

I liked starting the year with an exhibit about insects, some of them alive in small cages. Almost every child was immediately drawn to the caterpillars, grasshoppers, crickets, or whatever live creatures I was able to find for the beginning of the year; and they were interested in the display of wasp nests, insect skins, and other related nature finds. It gave the class a subject of wonder and conversation, something to help weld together a group of heretofore unrelated individuals. From the first day on, I was able to record by dictation from the children our daily observations on large chart paper, which we could read back.

First we had a Monarch caterpillar but it made itself a chrysalis. It's green and lean. It has gold lights. It is hanging on the top of the jar by a little black point. Maybe it will turn into a Monarch butterfly.

When the children were asked what they thought was happening inside the chrysalis, some of the answers were:

It's transforming into a butterfly.

It's just waiting.

I think the caterpillar is growing.

I think it's something special inside him that's learning to be a butterfly.

It's wondering when he's going to get out of the chrysalis because it's tight in there.

I think he's shy when there's a lot of kids.

I think it wants to get out because he wants to see the world and see the flowers.

I think it's having a good dream inside while it's turning into a very beautiful butterfly.

It's dreaming that when it comes out it wants a warmer place.

A saltwater tank that we kept in the room provided the children with material for observations, drawing, and writing during free-choice periods. Libby, who started off kindergarten as a reader and learned to write during the year, enjoyed acting as scribe for other children. Here is a collaboration recorded in December:

THE ONE [crab] WITHOUT THE SHELL IS FIAHTING [fighting]

THEH IS A YOLLE SNIAL [there is a yellow snail]

A HERMIT CRAEB IS JAMPING

THEH IS LOTS OF SPAK [sparkly] SHELLS

THEH IS A DIEMED [diamond]

THE CRAEBS ARE EATING THE SEAWEED

A MESEL SHELL MOTOHT IS WIHT [a mussel shell's mouth
is white]

Other children who were less inclined to write recorded their observations with pictures, sometimes dictating sentences or writing captions like SLTWTRTC [salt water tank]. I found that when we studied spiders in the class, children's journal stories often featured spider webs, just as caterpillars and butterflies appeared repeatedly in children's fantasies, drawings, and paintings throughout the year. Science study feeds children's imagination and aesthetic sense as much as it focuses their observational and logical powers, and it provides endless material for writing.

When the classroom offers both children and teachers freedom to choose and much time to pursue individual and group interests in depth, an amazing variety of writing styles, topics, and genres can arise even for beginning writers. Ruth had a poetic sensibility and thought in images:

De Firwz HAT De HOS wzz Bre De ThLren We SEE

[The fire was hot, the house was burning, the children were singing.]

Josh wrote factual material, usually on science topics:

A SNAKTHORMIG ACT ISN DAJRAS [A snake charming act isn't dangerous] BCAZ TAetR TACTE FAGS OWT [because they either take the fangs out] OR SO TLAPS TGATR [or sew the lips together]. SNAK THRMRS PLA SPATHL MYUSIC AND Te COBR SNACS dO SPATHL STF IN A BASCET. [Snake charmers play special music and the cobra snakes do special stuff in a basket.]

Reiko wrote fairy tales about princesses:

ONSAPONITIMDAWASAMOMENDBEIBEENDKISENDBYLIFLPLINSES [Once upon a time there was a mom and baby and kids and beautiful princess.]

Ella, a penguin lover, experimented with absurd stories:

A PNGN LKD THE NBR 9. HE DSID TWO MARE HR.
[A penguin liked the number 9. He decided to marry her.]

Aaron wasn't feeling well:

I HAV A COD IT MAKS MY NOS RAN SO FAST TAT I CAT CAS IT
[I have a cold. It makes my nose run so fast that I can't catch it.]

Rebecca wrote a continuing story about a QOEN [queen] in her journal, a sentence a day:

THE QOEN IS GOWING TO THE SOPRMIRKET
THE QOEN IS SOIMING IN TNE ROULD PIND [royal pond]
THE QOEN IS IN LOVE WITH A FLAOL [flower]

No matter what the children write, whether it's one-word labels (e.g., DNSR), a triumphant first sentence half copied from another source (i.e., "I LIKE KATZ"), an illegible story, a row of symbols, a correctly spelled journal entry, a cartoon with captions—it calls for appreciation and affords an occasion for showing the writing to the whole class. At any level of writing skill, children need to start thinking of themselves as writers, and their first attempts to break into the written code are exciting and a stimulus to other children.

When I interviewed some kindergartners near the end of the year about how they learned to write, the following are some of the responses:

You said that when you write words, don't ask the teacher how to spell it, "just sound it out." Before that, I was just asking people how to spell things. Now I don't have to ask people. I get bored when I ask people things. I can write everything. I sound it out. When I get stuck I just erase it and start again.

I have some words in my brain, and I think of them in my brain. Whenever I think of them it comes out of my brain and I write it.

I say it to myself in my mind, and then it goes down to my hand and then my hand writes it.

The children also told me that they learned from adults, other children, and books:

First my Mom told me. Then I put it in my head and remember.
Some of my friends taught me more writing because they knew more than me. In kindergarten my friends taught me all my writing.

I learned to write by listening to sounds and by people helping me. They just sort of told me some letters.

I learn from books. I take the book and look at the words I want to spell. If I found it in a book first, then I remember it for a whole week.

Throughout these interviews, I was both amused and pleased that none of the kindergartners credited their teacher with actually teaching them to write. They evidently considered themselves independent learners who had made good use of the human and material resources that school and home had to offer.

Not all children manage to write or read in kindergarten. Nor should we expect them to. But whatever children learn about literacy comes through a complex merging of many experiences, starting from much earlier in their childhood and continuing during school time. If we respect children's knowledge, abilities, and basic desire to learn to express themselves, we can allow them to explore writing in their own ways at their own pace. Writing will then become a natural extension of thinking, feeling, and speaking. The less we consider writing a "skill subject" to be taught by a specific method, and the more we open up to the infinite possibilities of written language, the more our kindergarten children will dare to take those challenging, determined, and wonderful first steps into literacy.

15

Unity in Diversity
Education Connections in Four Progressive
Education Frameworks

REBECCA E. DYASI AND HUBERT M. DYASI

I n this piece we discuss early educational experiences and go back to our young days in Africa, which prepared us to see value later on in the work of the North Dakota Study Group (NDSG). We discuss connections between those experiences and the educational principles and practices of the NDSG. The connections are not trivial; they have nourished and continue to be supportive of our professional interests and growth at critical times in our careers.

Informal Education

We grew up in different parts of Africa, Rebecca in Sierra Leone, and Hubert in South Africa. As a result, our experiences in and out of school, traditional African education and informal school education, differed but only in detail rather than in kind. In the informal and semiformal African education systems, we learned life skills through direct use of the knowledge and skills we were learning. Within the limits of age group responsibility, we participated in food production and preparation, in organization of public festivals, and in community events (e.g., real and mock weddings, settlement of disputes, etc.). Our knowledge of fauna and flora went beyond knowing their names to knowledge of characteristics, habits, and habitats. In our communities, children and adults alike constantly assessed that knowledge through questions such as, "How do you know it is that animal or that particular plant?" "Where do you find it?"

None of this was written; one had to remember it, but that was not an onerous task because everyone repeatedly encountered animals and plants in their daily lives and in the context of common conversations. We did not realize at that time that we were seriously cultivating awareness of the sequences and meanings of our activities, and of their vital connections to the building and sustenance of our communities. Later on, however, we greatly appreciated the educational value of learning through observation, participation, and understanding in socially constructed, public contexts.

Formal Schooling

The schools and colleges we attended were patterned after British academic traditions and were staffed by teachers and professors who themselves were products of English or European or American progressive education traditions. In these traditions, elementary and high school education focused on the development of the whole child and on engaging the child in active learning involving participation in individual and group activities. Although self-expression was valued, it was important that it be developed within a recognized socially constructed framework, with the school serving as a supportive socializing institution.

During college/university years, our studies in science included firsthand inquiry into nature. We were guided by scholars who themselves practiced firsthand science inquiry in their scholarly work and in their teaching. We loved that kind of science. We did not instantly associate our affinity for science inquiry with our early child-centered informal and formal education, but did when alerted by some of the senior students and professors. In science, for instance, we were learning to read, understand, and physically and intellectually manipulate nature in both the laboratory and field. Traditional African fishermen, who could neither read nor write, went on long fishing trips at night finding their way at sea by using stars as their map. Farmers too learned and understood the implications of seasonal changes for agriculture from direct experience. These activities have a qualitative resemblance to a meteorologist's who predicts weather from observations and measurements of air masses, temperature, humidity, and cloud formations. All of these acts are indicators of a complex, insightful understanding of the language of nature.

At university we were also educated to be teachers. We learned to move from theory to practice and back to theory. We used our practical learning experiences in science and our observations of children's learning as evidence for both theoretical scientific knowledge and knowledge of the profession of education. Our education in teaching and learning reinforced what we had already understood from our education in science—that scholars/teachers go on learning and improving their knowledge and practice throughout their careers.

Reforming Science Education in African Schools

Before the 1960s when most African countries were European colonies, some leading African scholars dreamed of a science education that would transform African education into a medium for young people to cultivate their individuality and develop their communities. An African philosopher, Rev. Solomon Caulker of Sierra Leone, expressed the dream at a science conference in Rehovoth, Israel, in 1960. Professor Jerrold Zacharias of the Massachusetts Institute of Technology (MIT) attended the conference and was exceedingly impressed by Rev. Caulker's ideas; he translated that dream into reality—a science education program in Africa. Known as the African Primary Science Program (APSP), it was administered by the Educational Services Incorporated (ESI), which later became Education Development Center (EDC).

The APSP developed inquiry-based science education materials and educational films for African schools, established or reinforced curriculum development efforts in African education institutions, and organized science education workshops and conferences. It also created lively communities of teachers; school administrators; senior officials of government ministries of education; and outstanding African, European, and North American progressive educators. The latter group included David and Frances Hawkins, Philip and Phylis Morrison, and Eleanor Duckworth, all of whom had been associated with the Elementary Science Study (ESS).

Five years after its founding, the APSP came under direct African administration as the Science Education Program for Africa (SEPA) with Hubert Dyasi as its executive director. SEPA expanded the APSP approach to all educational levels and established specialized centers on educational evaluation and on the education of teachers and teacher educators. In addition to producing teacher education materials, it developed inquiry-based science education programs in several countries and supported science teachers' networks. Rebecca Dyasi, who had worked with Charity James at the Goldsmith College of the University of London, directed one of the teachers' centers in Sierra Leone.

Connections with the Workshop Center at City College

From the early 1970s our work in Africa required us to visit the United States regularly to seek support and funding and to strengthen our professional links. On some of those visits we met with Lillian Weber and her staff at the Workshop Center. We had become aware of Weber's ideas and work through some of our staff in Africa, through friends such as Stanley Chu in New York, and from her connections with Alan Leitman of EDC. We instantly felt at home at the Workshop Center. Lillian Weber's ideas were very much in tune with ours; her work, like ours, focused on populations that had been poorly served by schools in terms of curricula, assessment, and academic success. During this early association with the Workshop Center, we understood the urgency of the struggle in this country against routinized teaching and learning practices and against excessive standardized testing of children in narrowly defined skills and facts. The connection with the Workshop Center ultimately led, in October 1984, to Hubert Dyasi's being appointed the Center's director.

In addition to carrying on the Workshop Center's activities in various areas (e.g., school development; serving as a case study of a college-based teachers' laboratory; leader teacher developer; educational conference organizer and publisher; and as a local, national, and state professional science education development resource; etc.), we further developed and refined the inquiry-based, student-centered model of professional education of teachers that Weber and her staff had started. In particular, we paid attention to teachers' acquisition of significant science concepts and methodology through firsthand study and documentation of phenomena of nature using principles of science inquiry (work that was later validated by inclusion in the National Science Education Standards and the New York State Mathematics, Science and Technology Learning Standards).

Together with teachers, we expanded the concept of teacher as inquirer into his or her own practice and as inquirer into children's learning in science. Teachers investigated natural phenomena, studied, discussed, and wrote critical reviews of research-based literature on inquiry learning for children. Center staff worked as co-professionals with teachers in their classrooms and supported their science and teaching investigations. As a result of participating in these and the Center's other workshop science education programs, teachers came to understand how people learn, how a person's knowledge deepens in relation to the degree of immersion in science inquiry, and the critical role teachers play in children's learning.

As they participated in the Center's long-term programs, teachers broadened their bases for assessing students' learning. They collected data on educational events in their classrooms and used them to facilitate their students' and other teachers' learning. The Center organized regular meetings of professionals and workshops at which teachers and sometimes children, parents, and assistant principals discussed the benefits accruing of school- and classroom-based communities of learners. The Workshop Center has published books, monographs, and science education videos and worked collaboratively with locally and nationally recognized academic and professional science institutions and organizations.

Connections with the North Dakota Study Group

Our initial experience of the North Dakota Study Group was in February 1985 when Hubert attended its annual meeting at Wingspread in Milwaukee, Wisconsin. What a thrilling, unforgettable, and inspiring educational experience it was! And every meeting we have attended has been a stimulating educational experience. What has struck us most about the Study Group is its consistent focus on, and support of, the creation and development of successful educational exemplars that translate belief and theory into practice, which in turn enriches belief and theory.

Over the years, a regular agenda item, Teachers' Voices, has expanded beyond classroom work to include broader issues such as equity, community involvement, and working with youth groups. The change has come about as a result of discussion and repeated self-examination of the NDSG as a model of unity in diversity, democracy, and social justice.

The NDSG's annual meetings draw participants from diverse age groups, educational experience, institutional affiliations, areas of specialization, geographical location, spheres of interest and social action, and race and ethnicity. The racial and ethnic mix of the annual meetings has changed dramatically over the years. Proportionately, the number of African Americans, Latinos, Native Americans, Asian Americans, and other "minority" groups who attend Study Group meetings is far higher than in the general population. But numbers by themselves can be of little significance if there is no direct participation by these groups in the organization's decision-making processes and if the decisions made on an inclusive basis are not honored by the organization, which is not the case with the NDSG. Judging by the stability and growth of its diverse membership, this group is successful in handling differing operational perspectives. Yet it continues to assess its development as a case study of harmonious unity in diversity in the implementation of successful progressive education ideas and practices.

Unity in Diversity Among the Frameworks

We see important underlying connections and continuities in the educational principles we have associated with four frameworks of our educational experience: traditional, informal African education; formal science education; science education development (SEPA and the Workshop Center); and the North Dakota Study Group.

All four frameworks represent translations of educational principles, beliefs, and purposes into successful educational and institutional practice. There is a clear belief in the significance of firsthand, inquiry-based learning and in the utilization of appropriate, rich social and physical contexts to support it. If students have a sense of ownership of the questions and inquiries they carry out, their motivation to engage themselves physically and intellectually with phenomena increases.

The nature and extent of evidence plays a critical role in all four frameworks of the educational experience. It may be valuable to engage in abstract conversations, but actual cases create bases for demonstrating what we say we know and how we know it, and for providing a broad, common platform for sense-making. Continual examination of documented cases also provides a broad array of sources of reliable evidence and enhances the chance that sound decisions and judgments will be made.

The concept of unity in diversity pervades the four selected frameworks: unity in human and educational values, in the respect for the intelligence of the teacher, in all children's capacity to learn, and in the continuity of learning.

16

Miriam's Standards

BRENDA S. ENGEL

Figure 16–1. *Drawing by Miriam in pencil on an 8½ by 11-inch piece of white paper, dated November 24, 1992.*

Born in December 1989, Miriam was just short of three years old when she made the drawing shown in Figure 16–1. It shows four figures identified (probably unnecessarily) in adult writing at the top of the paper—My Mom, Miriam, Sam, My Dad—and again at the bottom of the paper with the identifications written to the left of each figure. Clearly a family portrait.

The individual figures are drawn schematically—circles for faces, jagged waves representing hair, smaller circles for eyes, horizontal lines for mouths, another horizontal line for noses (except on the smallest figure of Miriam herself where the nose is omitted and the mouth is a narrow oval and "Dad's" face in which the mouth is obliterated by a darker scribble indicating a mustache). The bodies are elongated, vertical rectangles with horizontal lines protruding to either side indicating arms.

"Mom" is to the far left in the group: a rock-solid, square-ish presence conveying no-nonsense authority. The little scribbles attached to either side of her head probably denote earrings. Then comes Miriam, about a third her mother's size, looking rather mere. Next is Sam, Miriam's brother, almost twice her size in both height and width (although, in fact, he was only a little more than a year older). Finally there's "Dad"—significantly the tallest figure, leaning protectively sideways toward his family, his gender indicated by two long legs/trousers. The "togetherness" of the family group is reinforced by ten horizontal lines in the spaces between the figures, eight of them arms, two of them unexplained extras, all of them helping to "tie" together the array of figures.

With great economy of means and firmness of purpose Miriam has told us important (to her) facts and feelings about her family: their closeness as a group, their relative power as individuals, and her own place in this small hierarchy. Within the family lineup, she herself appears protected and safe. (It is notable that the arms extended laterally from each figure actually *touch* the neighboring figures—except for Sam's left arm which ends with a slight upward hook in space.)

There is something enviable about young children's unself-conscious, untutored directness of expression. The absence of the conventional constraints, which inevitably come with the complexities of more developed understanding, allows young children a kind of ease and freedom that, once lost, are gone forever. Paul Klee, an appreciator of child art, struggled to re-create the kind of immediacy of perception Miriam had at age three. He wrote in his diary, in 1905: "A good moment in Oberhofen. No intellect, no ethics. An observer above the world or a child in the world's totality" (Klee 1964, 190).

As children grow older, more experienced, and more aware of outside expectations, their work changes. No longer do arms protrude from halfway down the side of figures or eyes appear as empty circles. No one, however, has to tell children to "correct" their work, to revise their notions of proportions, or to add details. Somehow, in accordance with their own expanding awareness and ambition, they do add more details and elements of setting. They also make an attempt at conveying perspective, weight, and solidity. In fact, around the age of seven or eight children often strive toward a kind of realistic representation in their artwork that can lead to their becoming discontented and frustrated with their inability to measure up to their own standards. "I hate it! It doesn't look right! It doesn't look real!"

Standards? If these are standards held by children for their own work (and I think they are) where do they come from? Also, where have they been all this time, since infancy? They have, of course, been there—inside the child. Miriam's drawing is a serious, thoughtful representation of an intense personal interest: her family. She demands of herself both accuracy and completeness and presumably would not have been happy if she had left out one of the eight arms or some other crucial (to her) element. Accuracy and completeness, however, have to be understood within the context of a three-year-old's thinking and perceiving. A six-year-old's standards for completeness might include five fingers on each hand, centers in the eyes, eight ears and probably a suggested context in the form of a ground line and other selected elements of "scene."

These additions don't make the work better, only more age-appropriate. In other words, standards keep pace with age, experience, understanding, co-ordination, and other less obvious influences. They are adjusted (not *raised*) by the child according to his or her growing awareness, which begins with the infant's exclusive focus on the close-at-hand, usually caretakers and family members and objects in the immediate surroundings. With time, his or her awareness and interests expand to take in wider aspects of the social and physical worlds, a process that has probably been speeded up these days because of TV and other forms of rapid communication.

Very young children are not always interested in hearing others' evaluations of their artwork aside from a general desire for admiration and approval. They are usually more interested in their own experience of doing art, in which process is as important as product, than they are in the comments of others. Children's first critics, unless they (the children) have been singularly fortunate in having opportunities to do artwork at home, are likely to be their day-care providers or teachers. In progressive, child-centered settings, the adults observe and respond positively to children's work, calling attention to specific areas of interest or innovation. Their comments though, even when not intended to be evaluative, do communicate some sort of judgment through tone of voice, authenticity of reaction, degree of expressed enthusiasm, and the disposition they make of the work (put in a folder, hung on the wall, sent home, left in a corner). The teacher's responses weigh in with the child's own assessment of his or her work. Standards, which originally came only from inside the child, become at this point more public or communal, more open to the influence of others, including, in school, that of teachers and classmates.

In this process there is inevitably a giving-up—a giving-up of a measure of autonomy to outside influences. Miriam at age three would have been too involved in her own efforts and ambitions to pay much attention to suggestions or criticism from others. Older children become susceptible to outside opinion, with some children more inclined to cede authority than others. The aim, in progressive school settings, is to respect and encourage children's developing ability to look critically at their own work while, at the same time, taking into account the opinions of others—only to the extent, however, that these opinions make sense to the child. It is finally the child's intentions that lie behind and inform his or her standards for success.

If too much autonomy is given up by the child in the face of imposed standards, there is danger of banality, of producing boring artwork in obedience to someone else's ideas or routine prescription. One can, of course, see examples of this kind of banality in schools everywhere—in the rows of near-identical crayoned bunny rabbits at Easter or the formulaic cutout orange pumpkins at Halloween. The standards here, set by the teacher, have to do mainly with staying within the line, neatness, and faithfulness to the teacher's model, not with expressiveness.

Can there be no articulated, externally set standards for expressive work then—in the middle grades, high school, and college? I would say "probably not." Standards have to emerge from the work itself, not be prescribed in advance. Optimally they are recognized and perhaps articulated as the work is viewed by its creator and others—and the artist's own standards should outweigh all others. Picasso would never have invented cubism if he had conformed to the conventional canons of his day for figure or still life representations. His unshakeable belief in his own ideas and intentions gave him the courage to persist in the face of considerable criticism and derision

Since most children are more vulnerable than Picasso to the views of others, it is particularly important to support, to actively encourage, their ability to develop standards for their own work—ones that are consistent with their own ambitions and what they mean to express. When adults co-opt that function and set external standards, they deprive students of a measure of independence, self-confidence, and often motivation—of students' desire to achieve work that is in their own minds original, worthwhile, and satisfying.

There are, however, useful ways teachers and other adults can organize their observations of children's visual work by identifying broad areas for questions and attention. In a small book on child art, which I wrote some years ago (Engel 1995, 32), I suggested the following six areas:

1. *Materials, context*: What is it made of? And, if the information is available, when and under what circumstances was it made?

2. *Basic elements, techniques*: What can the observer see?

3. *Character of communication*: What does it represent?

4. *Aspects of organization, meaning*: How is the picture organized?
5. *Function, intent*: What is it about?
6. *Sources, origins*: Where does the idea come from?

These headings suggest only places to look, not what to look *for*.

Going back to the drawing of three-year-old Miriam, I described with some detail in the first paragraphs of this article the materials, elements, character of communication, organization, and meaning of the drawing. I could add, in area 6 of the preceeding list, that the idea clearly came from Miriam's experience of family life. This is the kind of close description that expands the viewer's understanding, relating it to the intentions of the creator of the work.

The standards Miriam seems to have set for herself might be described as: clarity, completeness, balanced composition, expressiveness (meaning) and economy of line. These qualities of Miriam's drawing, however, can't be held up as standards for the work of another three-year-old whose scribbly crayon drawing might, for instance, lack economy of line but effectively convey motion and excitement.

I have been discussing standards for children's expressive work. Do these ideas apply to their academic work, to reading, social studies, science, math? English educator Michael Armstrong wrote at the end of his classic work on children's learning: "We can observe [children's 'seriousness of purpose'] in their early writings, their art, their mathematics and their play; in every activity which absorbs them intellectually and emotionally" (1980, 206).

The issue then is how to extend this seriousness of purpose—so evident in the intense physical and intellectual strivings of infants and young children—into the elementary and high school years. How can we encourage students to continue to find interest in both creative and academic work? One step in that direction would be to allow them at least a major share in setting standards, encouraging their natural desire to become competent in the activities of the adult world they are joining.

What ordinarily happens, however, is that adults co-opt students' natural ambitions by becoming ambitious *for* them, setting external standards for academic achievement that effectively discourage students' own efforts. Teachers, administrators, and politicians then turn to substitute incentives—*carrots* such as grades, test scores, honors lists, and so on; and *sticks* such as retention, letters home, staying in for recess, withdrawing of privileges, and so on.

On the positive side, there is one relatively recent procedure being tried in some schools and school systems that is less demeaning to students than imposed standards: portfolios of student work as an assessment tool. Ordinarily the student, in consultation with teachers, selects the contents of the portfolio to represent his or her achievement in the various areas of the curriculum. The student then presents and defends the work before a committee made up of teachers, administrators, and often peers and/or community representatives. Assessment is of the evidence itself—the work—with the student taking the initiative in "making a case" for its adequacy. Various kinds of rubrics are in use to guide the assessment process—some of them more prescriptive than others. These usually identify areas for consideration, not unlike the six areas for observing children's visual art that I suggested before. In general, portfolio assessment gives students an active, creative role. (It is perhaps not a coincidence that "portfolios" were originally associated with art and artists.)

Returning then to Miriam, my hope for her is that she resist standards set exclusively by others, that she develop and maintain her own standards—through reflection as well as negotiation and discussion with friends, relatives, and teachers—and finally, that she continue to recognize, value, and act in accordance with her own "serious purposes."

17

Racing Through Childhood

DEBORAH MEIER

I have a picture in my head of what a good early childhood classroom might look like: a kindergarten ("children's garden") with color and light, open spaces and smaller cozy ones. There would be animals and plants, earth and water, books and pictures, plenty of natural and man-made materials. It would be a place where children would be drawn to explore, try out, investigate possibilities, invent, create new forms—and play. The "garden" would be populated by other children and adults, available for consultation and collaboration, also engaged in their own projects—serious or seriously playful.

From where do these images come—personal experience, imagination, history, or fiction? Have children lived in such near-ideal settings in the distant or recent past? Do they still, somewhere, in the present? There was a time when the worlds of home and work were not as separate as they are today. It was usual in agricultural societies, for instance, for children to share in adult tasks and still have a measure of independence for exploration and discovery. They lived alongside the adult world. Even the surrounds of my own childhood in the 1930s had some of the qualities of a "garden," which allowed us freedom to play with friends of many ages in the context of a familiar, safe neighborhood, with adults within easy call. The kindergarten in which I first taught was pale by comparison and not integrated among the generations, but it did at least offer children time, space, and materials. The early childhood classrooms I visited in England in the early seventies came closer to the ideal: children encouraged to initiate projects, allowed to move freely on their own between indoors and outdoors with adults from the neighborhood frequently supplementing the professional staff. One more example: the Reggio Emilia preschools in northern Italy, which I have read about, are carefully designed, materials-rich, aesthetically pleasing learning environments for largely low-income children. A central space in each school is designated the *atelier* (workshop). This space, shared by children and adults (including parents), is used for a variety of educational projects and art activities.

It is easy and tempting to romanticize other places and other times, easy to forget the abuses, hardships, and dangers faced by children under other circumstances. Yet the appealing images here, even if a bit romanticized, can serve to point up some of what has been lost in the current way in which we raise our young; what we seem to have for the first time, perhaps in history, abandoned along the way.

What then is missing these days? First of all, time and space for young children to play—unscheduled time and unorganized space that invite the child to improvise and invent. Second, the company of adults engaged in adult activities for authentic purposes—cooking, cleaning, reading, drawing, building, gardening, talking, adults conversing about adult matters. My argument, in short, is that children need both: time and space for childish pursuits as well as the company of adults engaged in adult work. Artists, carpenters, cooks, computer technicians, writers, farmers, scientists, engineers, as well as trades people, need to be working where children can observe, imitate, and learn from them—maybe even be helpful to them. Children need settings in which they too have authentic chores to do, suitable to their growing competence. In this country, these responsibilities and opportunities have been disappearing during our times.

One characteristic that distinguishes humans from other parent-loved mammals is the prolonged length of protected time they allow their children before they are expected to confront the demands and judgments of the adult world. Five years of such protection used to be a bare minimum and in some ways, and for some individuals, it lasted considerably longer. As Lillian Weber used to chide us impatient schoolteachers, "mother wit" seemed to know something about childhood that it has taken a long time for science to confirm. That "something" was play, stemming from the child's spontaneous and persistent interest in making sense of the world; imitative play as well as novel or inventive play, exercised within a protected space created by tolerant caretaking adults who were, at the same time, engaged in their own enterprises. The apparently random nature of children's early investigations of how things go together (and come apart) later evolve into more organized rule-constructed play.

The development of language is a case in point. Language first appears as a form of play— of imitation, invention, trying out, and observing the effects of experimentation. The brain's "capacity" to make language does not alone account for the ingenuity exercised by children in learning to speak, a skill practiced in the context of the nonjudgmental, forever forgiving, indulgent adults. In working out the details of language, the infant asks (and answers) which of all the possible sounds humans can make are used in her home tongue, which sounds work for a particular purpose, what intonation produces which response (questions, statements, demands, complaints), and the other subtleties of language that most children have mastered well before the age of five. All this, and much, much more, is achieved within the community created by an accepting family in which each child novice is presumed to be capable of becoming competent if largely left to his or her own devices.

As Frank Smith pointed out in *Understanding Reading* (1978), which we all read and argued over at NDSG meetings, children learn about ten new words a day if left to their own devices. In the typical school, we'd be lucky to formally teach ten a week, not to mention ten that stayed in their memory bank. Something about schooling reduces a child's likelihood of learning material of comparable complexity efficiently, and apparently effortlessly. Experts today speak as though it was not natural to learn, that preschool must help little ones "learn" to learn—hence the focus on "readiness" skills.

In schools we are in fact losing two important sources of learning: the child's world of play and inquiry and children's familiarity with the world of engaged, skilled adults and somewhat older peers. Maybe the ideal images I presented at the start of this article are too far removed from present reality, lost causes, "pie in the sky" and thus an invitation to pessimism. Changes in the life of families and the workplace have made early childhood very different. The introduction of the mass media and the world of advertising into the home life of very young children complicates it still further. Nonetheless, pointing out what is being lost in most present-day educational institutions, as well as in life at home, may help us think about what could be done to restore, whenever and wherever possible, at least some positive elements of an earlier version of infancy.

The losses have been coming on us gradually. Children's natural ways of learning the world—through exploration, invention, and imitation—have been traded in for mandated curriculum, direct instruction, and prescribed standards backed up by the authority of the state and measured by standardized testing. There were, of course, early warnings of the direction education was taking. When the NDSG gathered that first time in 1972, at Vito Perrone's invitation, it was in response to these new and gathering threats to two promising federal programs—Head Start and Follow Through. Maybe the very name, "Head Start," should have warned us of what was ahead—the sense of education as a race.

Head Start, begun in the mid-sixties, was designed to help poor children "catch up" to middle-class children. With it the idea of early schooling as a *garden* was disappearing. The image of education as a race was substituted at an ever-earlier age. In fact, the adults closest to the child were often seen to be the obstacle to academic success, they themselves in need of teaching about how to be good influences on their own children. Now the idea was that, with the help of middle-class teachers and a proper middle-class curriculum (trips to zoos; letter recognition; reading good books; learning colors and numbers; and learning to share, raise their hands, and stand quietly in line), poor children would enter kindergarten or first grade on a par with their competitors "ready to learn." (Note the presumption again that before school they hadn't been learning.)

President Johnson's War on Poverty was meant to narrow the gaps between the rich and the poor. The U.S. Office of Education introduced several legislative initiatives to that end. But when federal monies were involved, legislators thought they needed to know whether the efforts were working. Were Head Start, and later Follow Through, really closing the gaps between advantaged and disadvantaged children? There were many competitors for the honor of sponsoring the one "best way"—from advocates of direct instruction of academic skills to advocates of child-initiated play, with a host of in-betweens and variations. And, of course, in the controversy over how to determine what works best, descriptive and qualitative methods of assessment were deemed unacceptable and "hard data"—numerical measurement by tests—became the standard.

When I taught Head Start in Philadelphia in 1965, we gave a pretest (September) and posttest (June) to see whether kids were mastering their shapes, colors, alphabet, and so on. That was all and it seemed to be enough to satisfy Congress. Later, as federal intervention increased, pressure grew to identify "the one best way" based on standardized test results. A massive protest by parents and child-development advocates put a temporary stop to the testing mania but the idea of finding the *best way* periodically reemerged, and along with it test scores as the significant data.

One could see the shape of things to come. Despite ups and downs in an uneven history, the thrust over the last forty years has been to start schooling ever earlier—and not just for poor people's children—and to measure children by standard paper-and-pencil tests focused on standard "school" skills (and again, not only poor children). This despite the fact that substantial evidence noted that test reliability was statistically very low the younger children were. Most pre–post testing programs were, furthermore, carried out consistently for only a year or two, thus ignoring side effects and long-term consequences. (Only one significant longitudinal study was conducted—the High Scope project.) In the meantime, the expected level of kindergarten skills was simply reset to match those previously taught in first grade, while the measure of prekindergarten was raised accordingly. Today, children are deemed not ready for kindergarten if they don't know what the average six-year-old child was expected to learn in early first grade twenty-five years ago! (And which in Finland, with the highest reading levels in the world, isn't introduced until children are seven years old!)

As kindergarten became the norm—appearing less and less as a children's garden—what was happening to family life? Children were keeping less and less company with adults engaged in adult occupations. I was first concerned about this when I became involved with secondary school kids and realized how the closer they came to adulthood, the fewer adults they knew well. It came as a surprise then to realize when I returned to working with younger children, that this was happening at both ends of the spectrum of childhood. Even when children were at home—and annually the amount of such time has gradually but steadily decreased—busy, overworked parents were anxiously trying to prepare their children to meet the standards set by the school.

The schools' pedagogy and curriculum have become the preferred mode of "instruction" at home as well as at school. Flash cards, early learning-to-read books, and other skills-oriented activities (often mislabeled *academic*) are fed to children by dutiful parents and caretakers to ensure that they are ready for the race. The more natural forms of home teaching and learning have become obsolete—less oral exchange, once common in the dialogue between parents and young children. Even normal household chores are less frequently assigned to children as their useful roles within the family decrease. These have been replaced by direct instruction (children asked to read and respond to prescribed questions), formal counting games, and other commercial "teaching" tools. TV and the computer are the tools of choice. Families are swamped by well-meaning books and articles about how they should mimic the school's agenda and style to help prepare their children for school success.

The impact of the popular media on young children cannot be overstated. The advertising industry has stepped up its effort to shape the ideas and desires of even one-year-olds—away from simple open-ended toys that require imagination and initiative. In *Consuming Kids* (2004), Susan Linn describes the ruthless corporate strategies to turn children into early consumers. Child psychologists are hired to figure out how to strengthen babies' desires in ways that undermine family and school authority (e.g., to test out the degree of whining and nagging that parents can tolerate before they give in). Schools, instead of being a powerful antidote to such well-funded efforts, too often either parody them or present such a pale alternative as to increase their lure.

This is not a case of simply not having the resources to do otherwise. It's a conscious plan of action. Middle-class children, in spite of their presumed advantages (more educated parents with more available time), are subjected to similar pressures. I spent time a year ago watching a richly funded, academically sponsored preschool program for professional families in which every child spent three hours in a group of no more than two or three peers under the direct supervision of a trained adult manipulating children's games, materials, and toys. Each child and each piece of material was designed for a single cognitive purpose, and his or her IEP (individualized educational plan) was regularly updated. One-way glass allowed parents to watch and learn what they should be doing more of at home. I saw neither tears nor joy, just relentless pursuit of adult-designed goals. When asked about "creativity," the director assured us that some children's IEPs included that and materials were offered to respond to such needs. It wasn't for lack of money! (The only bright spot was the one Head Start class where a tradition of children's play still prevailed.)

Is this early programmatic instruction at home, at school, and in the media causing something else to be forced out, something critical to the health of our species, something fundamental to our capacity for coping with the world in a humane and creative way? This capacity may be even more essential in a world where change occurs more rapidly than ever before. A study conducted in Florida by Rebecca Marcon, reported on in a major research journal, suggests that deprivation of imaginative opportunities and play may be harmful even in the most limited school sense. A six-year study of a random sample of four-year-olds who attended three different kinds of preschools in the same school district showed startlingly different results. Children in the more directed, academic style preschool had somewhat better results in kindergarten on standard school tasks but worse on social behavior. By fourth grade, the children who had spent that one year in the program designed around child-initiated activities had outperformed the others in both academic and social tasks.

Although some insist that despite its risks such a regimen is the only way to close the gaps between rich and poor, this would only make some logical sense if we could withhold such advantages (plus) from the rich. In fact, test-oriented approaches exacerbate the mismatch between home and school that undermines the natural strengths of most children of low-income homes. While in an increasingly unequal society no program of schooling can be expected to undo the damage of poverty, some forms of early childhood support can do a better job of maximizing all children's strengths (see the results of the Marcon 2002 study). By celebrating what even the most economically and socially disadvantaged come with, not just what they are missing, we undercut social status differentials rather than increase them.

When I feel most despairing I am buoyed up by my daily experience of the resiliency of children. I was happy to discover that even in the year 2000 little kids, at recess, are still digging holes to China, creating fairy castles in backyard bushes, and inventing all manner of imaginary worlds when left to their own resources. There is no way, however, to get conclusive evidence about the price society and its children may be paying for the loss of childhood; but, there are good reasons to be even more alarmed than we were during the seventies. As we place greater reliance on institutional care for young people from early infancy to well into their twenties, the consequences of schooling policies become even more crucial. This remains true even though the other primary educator—the mass media—has grown far more powerful and may already have greater influence than schools over children's views of the world and its values. The increasingly dry, controlling, programmatic schools, along with curtailed home life and the pervasive, seductive influence of the media, have together usurped the traditional invitation to children to join the world of adults. This "joining with" (in Lillian Weber's words) is a form of education we may be abandoning to our peril—disastrously if a central purpose of education is conceived as preparing the young for full membership in a community of equals.

PART FIVE

Teachers and Teacher Preparation

Progressive educators and progressive schools respect teachers as potentially creative, intelligent, and trustworthy guardians of children's welfare and education. Rather than being constrained by prescribed methodologies and scripted curricula or threatened by the outcomes of high-stakes standardized testing, teachers can be truly responsible and thoughtful about the children in their care.

Helen Featherstone writes from personal experience about the crucial importance of respecting and listening seriously to learners on all levels—from teachers of teachers and classroom teachers to children in classrooms. Diane Mullins gives an account of her own unusual, inclusive, democratic classroom-as-community. She exemplifies respect as an active reaching out to, and learning from, the experience of others, often of different ages and backgrounds. Eleanor Duckworth writes about the relationship between the world and the learner/scientist: the excitement and deep satisfaction that come from both teachers and students using mind and imagination to explore the "reality to which each belongs."

Leslie Alexander's chapter opens with the resonant sentence, "The power in a classroom lies in the autonomy of teacher voice." Her story of the Muscota New School, a teacher collaborative, exemplifies the educational benefits of respecting and trusting teachers' intelligence and serious intentions. It is also the only direct account in this book of a "small school"—a movement that has been important to progressive education. Small schools have built-in possibilities for flexibility, responsiveness to need, and attention to individuals (staff and children all know each other well).

The Philadelphia Teachers' Learning Cooperative, during its twenty-five-year history as a voluntary, informal (though structured) group, has supported its members in maintaining progressive, democratic values in the midst of an alien system. The three authors of this chapter, Rhoda Kanevsky, Lynne Strieb, and Betsy Wice, have been instrumental in introducing to the Cooperative methods of observation, reflection, and recordkeeping developed at the Prospect Center in Vermont (see article by Patricia Carini in Part VI of this book).

18

Learning Progressive Teacher Education

HELEN FEATHERSTONE

In 1991, I became very interested in approaches to teaching elementary mathematics that involved children in investigating nonroutine math problems, in presenting their ideas to one another, and in working together to understand one another's solution strategies—teaching that emphasizes reasoning and sense-making, connections between mathematical ideas, representing, and communicating. While observing in the third-grade math class taught by my friend and colleague Deborah Ball, I became fascinated by children's mathematical ideas. Reading the *Standards* volumes published by the National Council of Teachers of Mathematics (1989, 1991), I saw new complexities in the intellectual work children needed to do in order to understand arithmetic.

In 1995, I began to teach Teaching Mathematics to Diverse Learners (TE-402) to seniors in Team 1, one of three elementary teacher education programs at Michigan State University. Most of my students had learned math in fairly traditional classrooms where being "good at math" meant recalling multiplication facts quickly and solving computation problems correctly. As their teacher, I was excited about offering them new images of mathematics. I was an evangelist, eager to convince prospective teachers of the merits of this new approach. Many of my students, however, greeted the unfamiliar ideas with skepticism, arguing that children would fail on standardized tests if they did not memorize algorithms and practice computation each day.

In class we discussed readings, watched videos of teaching, and tackled math problems together—problems that challenged college seniors but could also, if adapted, engage elementary school students. My students enjoyed working together on these problems and the experience persuaded some that this approach to math teaching might have merit. However, others left the course feeling that they had spent a semester learning about an approach to math teaching that simply would not work in ordinary classrooms. As a teacher educator, I often felt frustrated and unsuccessful.

I spent much of 1999 studying the role of play in the learning of children. In December, when I sat down to revise my TE-402 syllabus, I had begun to think hard about the potential role of play in the learning of college students. So, along with the questions I considered every year—How can I help students to feel that teaching that takes account of students' thinking is possible in the schools in which they expect to teach? How can I help them learn to listen to and appreciate children's mathematical ideas? How can I help them get more out of their efforts to teach lessons to small groups?—I was asking, "How can I help these seniors to see possibilities for intellectual play in math and math teaching?"

The day before the first meeting of the course, I put this question to Dirck Roosevelt, a colleague with whom I was exploring research on play (and a longtime member of the NDSG); his response caught me off balance. That evening, I wrote in my teaching journal:

> The most important thing Dirck said today, the most profoundly helpful to my efforts to figure out where I go wrong, where I might do better at this teacher education thing was that . . . when . . . he did not feel at all like teaching, he found it helpful to remind himself that he really was curious about how these students thought about things. . . . I thought (and said) that I thought that my attitude had often been less open and interested— [more of] a missionary impulse to convert them to a better way of teaching math . . . I think I haven't truly been curious and open (often not even close) although I have tried to seem that way, to make the classroom safe for all ideas.
>
> I think if I want people to play with ideas I do need to cultivate this genuine curiosity. . . .

Because of this conversation with Dirck, I resolved to cultivate my own curiosity about the students' ideas in the semester ahead.

Four Days with the Students

The next day, Monday, TE-402 met for the first time. My teaching journal noted that several activities had not gone quite as I had hoped they would, but concluded: "I did feel [today] much more open and curious and even affectionate [toward the students]. . . . It felt good."

My account of Tuesday's class is saturated with pleasure in the students and in all they had done with the activity I had planned.

We did the horse-trading problem[1] and the participation was very animated and cheerful, and a quite lovely thing happened: For the first time ever (and I have done this problem on the first day quite a few times), all those who reported answers/ways of doing the problem had the right answer. I was astonished. Two people explained what they did and others said they had done pretty much the same. Both solutions were simple and straightforward. I asked if anyone did anything different and no one said they had.

So I said, "This is the first time I had ever had a class agree on an answer, and if you use this problem in your fourth grade, you will probably not have everyone agree. So what I would like you to do is try to imagine how someone might get a different answer . . ." And Miranda raised her hand and said, "Well, I know how they might get a different answer, because I did!!!" And she explained her way and it sounded very reasonable, and then others said that they had done what she did but when they heard Cheryl's solution it made so much sense that they decided it must be right. (And I got to point out that we should all be really grateful to Miranda for being brave and saying this because it was a vivid demonstration of how hard it is to create a culture/environment where people feel comfortable having a way of thinking about the problem that they think is probably wrong.)

And then four other people explained how they got $10 (wrong answer) and why it made sense to them. . . . It seemed that although most of the four to five dissenters had decided that $20 was right because it made sense (and probably because so many people had gotten it), none could see any logical or mathematical flaw in their earlier solution. I sent everyone off to write a few sentences on how they solved the problem and how someone who got a different solution solved it and how they would convince the person who got the different solution that their solution was right. I was (obviously) very pleased.

Wednesday I took the entire class to visit a second/third-grade class (recommended, once again, by Dirck) in an urban school about a twenty-minute drive from the university. I had arranged this visit because for the rest of the semester my students would be observing and teaching small groups in a school in an affluent and almost entirely white suburb; I wanted them to see that it was as possible to teach math in progressive ways in schools serving poor children and children of color as in affluent suburbs[2].

The lesson was wonderful. After the teacher, Patricia Pricco, presented the four related problems, the children worked alone and in pairs (and with the visiting students) for about twenty minutes and then, when the class reconvened, listened eagerly as their classmates presented different solutions to these problems. Several cheered when Pat called for solutions to the last and hardest problem and one declared, "That was the *bestus* problem."

When we met on campus on Thursday—and later, when I read what they had written—I learned how much, and why, the prospective teachers had enjoyed the visit. More than three-quarters of them wrote or spoke with deep appreciation of the kind, supportive, and respectful way the children listened to their classmates. Many were also delighted to see second and third graders *enjoying* math so much and inventing so many ways to solve the math problems (more, several observed, than they themselves had seen). And they wrote feelingly about how much they learned from finally *seeing* the sort of discussion they had read about throughout their program.

I wrote three jubilant single-spaced journal pages about the next part of our discussion—a follow-up to the horse problem. Here I was delighted by the intensity of their attention to one another's ideas, by the courage of those who repeatedly asked for help in understanding others' strategies, by the connections they saw between our discussion and the one in the class we visited. My journal account concluded:

> So, what made all of this possible? Certainly it wouldn't have happened if Miranda hadn't come out of the closet on Tuesday with her $10 solution. I think the example of Pat P's students loving doing math together and listening so thoughtfully to one another's ideas played a part. Barb's game. Jennifer's enactment. All of these moved us forward when we could have gotten stuck. Genuine curiosity is surely central: People really wanted to figure this out—whatever "this" was for them. And what about my curiosity?

I ended this first week feeling excited about my students and the semester ahead. Nor was I disappointed. Throughout the term, the students engaged enthusiastically with the reading, the weekly writing, and with the projects; the lessons they taught in the elementary school satisfied me and them more than those taught in previous semesters; in their teaching reports, they described their students' problem-solving strategies in detail—they had learned to inquire into children's thinking.

What the Teacher Educator Learned

This experience changed the way I worked as a teacher educator. I learned some important lessons and relearned others.

First, I learned that just as I cannot teach children well unless I am interested in their thinking, I cannot teach prospective teachers well unless I am curious about their ideas[3]. I also learned that such curiosity is self-perpetuating; for example, fascinated by all they said about Pat Pricco's students' thinking, I listened with added interest to their ideas about the horse problem. I had, in the past, been far more interested in converting my students to a particular view of math teaching than in exploring their ideas. I had failed at curiosity, and this failure had had important consequences for my teaching practice. In the introduction to this book, Brenda Engel identifies "belief in children's serious mindedness and serious intent" as a value undergirding the work of the NDSG; progressive teacher education respects the serious mindedness of prospective teachers.

Second, I learned that participating in one wonderful lesson where the children treat each other kindly and are clearly enjoying learning will accomplish a great deal even if students' other field experiences are pedestrian. To learn, prospective teachers, like elementary schoolchildren, need experiences that involve them physically and emotionally as well as intellectually. Fortunately, one such experience can accomplish a great deal: My students referred back to the visit to Pat Pricco's class throughout the term, using it to describe and make sense of what they saw elsewhere.

Third, I learned to enjoy doing teacher education. Throughout the semester—and for nearly all semesters since—I could hardly wait to get to class on Wednesdays, and I left each class pondering points made in the discussion. We talk too little about the importance of pleasure in teaching: The Puritan hangover makes pleasure here seem almost indecent. However, I work hard to convince my students that children's mathematical ideas are interesting and that exploring these ideas is both exciting and educational. I teach this best when I am enjoying my own teaching.

My experiences with TE-402 in spring 2000 also reminded me of some things I already knew but had perhaps put out of my mind.

First, because we know far less than we need to know to accomplish the goals of progressive teacher education, teacher educators in progressive programs must keep talking and asking questions. Had Dirck not set me to thinking about the need for curiosity in *all* teaching, and if he had not steered me toward Pat Pricco's class, my students and I would have learned far less. Fortunately, as members of the Steering Committee of Team 1, which met every two weeks to address problems of all sizes and set new directions, Dirck and I were part of an ongoing conversation about practice. (Four other members of the Team 1 Steering Committee—David Carroll, Susan Donnelly, Jay Featherstone, and Sharon Feiman-Nemser—were also members of the NDSG.) The dialogue helped us all to understand the entire program, not just the courses for which we were individually responsible, and it created opportunities for analyzing problems of practice that none of us could solve alone.

Second, progressive teacher education must aim to support the development of new professional identities; to do this it must provide prospective teachers with good models. Nationally (and at MSU), most teacher candidates are white women from middle-class families whose public school classmates looked much like them; most expect to teach in similar schools. In Team 1, we aimed to deepen prospective teachers' awareness of social inequalities and to foster the skills and dispositions needed for successful teaching in urban schools. In order to persuade college students that they can survive and thrive in high-needs schools, we must show them urban classrooms in which children are enjoying intellectual challenges and supporting one another's explorations.

After the visit to Pat's classroom, many of the TE-402 students wrote that they now had a vision of the kind of math class they would like to create, that they realized that they had much to learn, but that they were willing to put in the time because the goal excited them so much. At the end of the semester, six of the twenty-six students identified their visit to Pat's class as the experience that had influenced their learning the most.

In an effort to explicate the basis of moral behavior, Immanuel Kant argued that it was never moral to treat another human being as a "means": Human beings must be seen and treated as ends in themselves. Good K–12 teachers instinctively obey this rule: Their work with students, whether first graders or high school seniors, is undertaken for the good of these children or adolescents and not to accomplish a goal external to their well-being.

As I have reflected on the meanings of my TE-402 story, I have come to feel that there is a pitfall in the work of teacher education. Like me, most of my colleagues became teacher educators because they were dissatisfied with U.S. schools and hoped to have some positive impact on at least a few of them. Because we no longer teach in public schools ourselves, the prospective teachers in our classes represent our best hope of improving schools. Despite our best intentions, we find ourselves in a position that Kant has advised us to see as problematic: Our students have become, at least partly, a means to an end—improved opportunities for *their* future students—rather than an end in themselves. This difficulty was, I think, at the heart of the problem I was facing in January 2000.

Kant asks us to think hard about how our purposes as teacher educators connect to the students who are actually in our classrooms. To me, this story is about what happened when I took multiple steps that closed the distance between me and my students, putting myself in a position to hear their thoughts and to see their points of view. My new position allowed me to do a better job of connecting my students' purposes to our work together. When this happened, I looked and felt more like an educator and less like an evangelist. I also made more converts.

Notes

[1] The horse-trading problem: "A man bought a horse for $50 and sold it for $60, then bought it back for $70 and then sold it for $80. What was the financial outcome of this transaction? Did he make $20 or $10, or $0, or did he lose $20 or $10?"

[2] Because my section had been assigned for their weekly field work to a school in an affluent and almost entirely white suburb and because in 1998 several students had concluded that "you can do this kind of teaching in the suburbs, where children know their facts and know how to behave, but in urban schools you have to teach traditionally," I decided that during the first week of the course, when we would be together for four mornings (during the rest of the semester we would meet on campus once a week and spend another morning in an elementary classroom), I would arrange a visit to an urban classroom where math was taught progressively and where most of the students were African American. I asked Patricia Pricco (also at Dirck's suggestion) if she would be willing to have my twenty-five seniors visit her second/third-grade class. She agreed to the visit and arranged to talk to the seniors both before and after the math lesson, explaining her reasons for teaching as she did, laying down rules for the seniors' participation, and answering their questions.

[3] Vivian Paley, in a lovely essay about the evolution of her thinking and teaching practice (1986), describes a moment of truth in which she realized that—both as a Great Books discussion leader with adults and as a preschool teacher—although she had always solicited the ideas of her learners and tried earnestly, as the discussion leader, to connect these ideas, she had never actually been *interested* in what her students had to say. I have always found this piece both powerful and instructive, and have worked hard to teach prospective teachers to listen carefully to their students' ideas, so I was both surprised and embarrassed to realize that I had not myself been especially interested in my students' thinking.

19

The Classroom
Connection and Community

DIANE K. MULLINS

L earning, teaching, and growing is a lifelong adventure. I am able to get a better sense of it, and thereby of myself, by viewing it from different perspectives—those of adults as well as of children.

I have been a New York City schoolteacher for more than thirty years and, for all but a few of them, worked in one public school in lower Manhattan. Ingrid was in my first class, in 1972, a second grader in the combined second/third/fourth grade. I've been in touch with her and her family throughout all the intervening years.

On a recent evening I had occasion to walk to the theatre with Ingrid, now a Ph.D. candidate in computer science. Before that, she had been teaching at my school, PS 3, and then, for a bit, ran her own company. I told her about the chapter I was asked to write about the North Dakota Study Group, of which I had been a longtime member. My thoughts strayed to parents, narrative reports, trips, classroom experiences, and other school matters. Ingrid said, "Write about the children or a child. There's too much talk about teachers and staff development and parents and money. Focus on the child."

And so I chose to write about John, whose life in school involved his mother, grandmother, his friends, his intense interests and abilities—all against the backdrop of his second country, language, and culture.

I remember the day John came to class with his mother and grandmother. Registering for school was evidently a formidable experience for his mother, Robin, so her mother led the way. In order to feel confident that this was a place in which John could feel comfortable, both women spent much of that day at the school. John had previously been homeschooled, then attended a one-room school on an island in southern Greece.

John's interests and images were associated with the landscape of his Greek island—fish, tides, crustaceans, and the foliage of the beach. He drew the objects and scenes that he knew. An astute observer, John captured, examined, and recorded his memories. In essence, he drew what he still held inside him. John's father, I found out, was a visual artist with a remarkably accurate eye and hand, his work patient and clear. John's own quiet concentration and deep engagement were of the same quality as his parents'.

John's first written stories were in Greek. After a while he began a few sentences in English, then he went on to writing only in English. At home, his mother read to him—among other books, *Dr. Doolittle,* which he loved listening to. During the two years John was in my class, he was away a good deal. During a six-month stay in Greece with his family, he wrote me letters about his experiences and adventures (for example, see Figure 19–1).

Coming to school was, for John, a choice. His parents made it clear to him that he could stay home—be homeschooled—if he chose. Thinking back, I realize returning to school was always a choice for me too. There was the option of not coming back, even when I didn't take it up. Perhaps it should be an option for all who attend schools—children and teachers alike.

In class John spent time with Yuki, who had been born in Japan. She concentrated on learning about the other children, learning to know New York, and learning its language. Yuki's mother and a friend spent two weeks in our classroom. They too were learning the language, the rhythm of English, and the ways of New York children. When Casey joined the class in mid-year, John also became his special friend. John was able and willing to talk about his out-of-school life and experiences in this new relationship with Casey. Casey learned to converse in ways not available to him before. Casey and John "grew" one another. They developed a kind of confidence between them that invited classmates to join in. They constructed things and worked with electricity. They imagined and then represented their imaginings in two or three dimensions. Some of their activities depended on their cooperation. Probably neither one of them would have been able to accomplish what they did without the other. They spent time at each other's homes and became virtually part of each other's families.

From her first hesitant school entrance, John's mother, Robin, became active in the school community. Before the Fortieth Anniversary of the United Nations when most of our children participated in the Thousand Cranes celebration, Robin came to class and taught us origami. Her mother, John's grandmother, showed us slides of the Memorial Peace Park in Hiroshima, which inspired us to make our own cranes, which we sent to the Peace Park. Robin continued to be a vivid presence in the school when her second child, Peter, joined the community. She was the central, persistent, and eventually victorious figure in the struggle to have gates installed on the windows of our

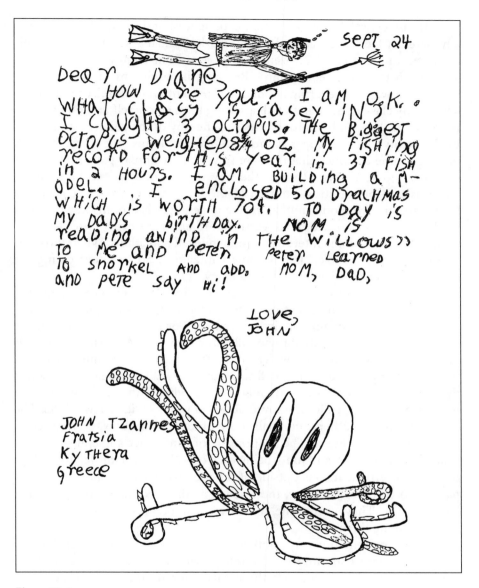

Figure 19–1

old building. She shared with us her passion for George Washington—both during and well after the time her children were enrolled in our school. She shared and eventually donated much of her shell collection to us. She continued coming to class to show the children the picture books she was writing and to seek their perspective for books she was reviewing.

In my classroom the activities, experiences, and views of adults, usually parents, have been central to my work—which I see as helping children become responsible citizens in the classroom community and, later, activists in the wider community. Bringing in adults, making their work visible, is a way of preparing children for present and future social responsibility. My classroom is first of all a setting to meet oneself and others. I try to make this happen by putting things in the way of the children and adults in the room (like the paper cranes). Often people become aware of each other or come to notice that they are traveling on similar paths.

I try to keep myself out of the way when that seems to be useful—which is not the traditional notion of the teacher. My sense is that people learn naturally from one another. In the mixed-age classrooms in which I've worked, it's easier for people to reach toward another's experience. The curriculum is based on the interests of both children and adults. When those interests are made visible, they become contagious. So too does caring for others and a sense of justice and democracy.

Another aspect of what we do has to do with experience outside the classroom. Children are able to see each other in different ways, in new settings, able to feel a quality of "in-chargeness." For many years we began the year with a trip to what used to be called the New York Aquarium. The children themselves figured out which subway to take and how much it would have cost to travel had we not had the subway pass. The Aquarium was just the right size, bounded so children became familiar with the layout. As with most trips we took, children moved about in groups with a few adults. The proximity to each other among all those others in the subway gave them a feeling of connectedness. (The relationship of confidence and connectedness is illustrated by Casey and John: being each other's "confidant" led to feelings of confidence.) Excursions outside of school also provide opportunities for parents to come to trust me, the teacher, as they see their children in the larger world. They also come to know each other—a connectedness is formed among them.

Public presentations are another way children connect with each other in the classroom community. Children present something they have been working on to the group, something that interests them—an experience, piece of writing, homemade game, map project, a construction, artwork, music, or dance. It could be a work in process. The presentation is followed by questions or comments from the other children. This daily occasion allows interests to come to the fore and connections made to members of the class, who respond, perhaps asking about some particular aspect of the sharing about which they're curious. The process of public presentation serves to establish standards, which children develop for themselves, about the quality of the work they do and choose to share with their classmates.

Since it is impossible to be "the teacher" to a room full of children, I make it clear that I am only one of many "teachers" in the classroom. The teaching, learning, and growing among us is a shared responsibility. I hope this understanding is carried out in the lives these students lead long after they have left the classroom. I see my work as helping people notice and appreciate their own interests and those of others. Children find one another and group themselves around intriguing questions that they themselves develop.

When children have the opportunity to talk with one another, walk with one another, listen to one another, working together toward something larger than themselves becomes possible. As Lillian Weber emphasized, being in an intergenerational surround is essential. Classrooms, and the grouping of children, can become vital intergenerational settings. Perhaps here people can, together, come to value their own humanness and learn to express it in large human ways.

As the years go by, past and present blend. Yuki and John still have a deep friendship. I saw Yuki recently on my way to a meeting of the NDSG. She's an artist studying at the Art Institute of Chicago. John, with his kayak, continues to fish. And Ingrid, who is now an adult professional and my adviser on what to write about, is at the same time the little girl who was in my class in 1972—very small, long straight hair, bright attentive eyes, full face, alert, curious, social, and as talkative as I remember. Ingrid was the smallest and put great energy into finding out about her classmates. She participated in the dramatic play and constructions of this particular group of children but was also drawn to science and math. Now Ingrid serves as my guide to computers and continues to be teacher and friend. In many ways she is a reference for me. She is a marker of time.

20

A Reality to Which Each Belongs

ELEANOR DUCKWORTH

The fundamental factors in the educative process are an immature,
undeveloped being; and certain social aims, meanings, values incar-
nate in the matured experience of the adult. . . . It is easier to see the
conditions of their separateness, to insist upon one at the expense of
the other, to make antagonists of them, than to discover a reality to
which each belongs (1956, 3).

—JOHN DEWEY
THE CHILD AND THE CURRICULUM

In *The Child and the Curriculum,* Dewey goes on to say:

> There is no sheer self-activity possible—because all activity takes place in
> a medium, in a situation, and with reference to its conditions. But again,
> no such thing as an imposition of truth from without . . . is possible. All
> depends upon the activity which the mind itself undergoes in responding
> to what is presented from without. (1956, 30–31)

So how do we present material "from without" so that the activity that "the
mind itself undergoes" is valuable? That is the challenge of making
curriculum.

During the weeklong conference in 1962 that launched the curriculum development program known as the Elementary Science Study, various
people had ideas about how curriculum should be organized: around
ecology—conserving the resources of the planet; around physics, the foundation of all the sciences; around the developmental psychology of children's
thinking; around astronomy or some other discipline. Each of these organizing frameworks seemed fine; none seemed compelling.

After that week of discussion, with no agreement reached as to an organizing frame, teams went to work—in laboratories and with children. And then the curriculum started. Not grand ideas, but looking for pieces that worked—pieces that engaged children in thinking about things that the scientists loved.

That was an early revelation for me—how much the scientists loved their subject matter. I remember discussing this with a literary friend— how astonished he was to read, in scientists' comments on their work with and for kids, so much passion for their subject matter. And even more surprising, that was what they wanted to share. They wanted to make curriculum that would engage kids and teachers in their—the scientists'—own passions.

That meant, of course, engaging kids and teachers in the details of the subject matter: seeing on film the dividing of a greatly magnified frog egg as cell lines formed and multiplied, visible indentations on the pudgy brown egg; "tuning" the strings of two pendulums until they would make 50 swings back and forth without getting out of sync, or until one would make exactly 3 swings, say, while the other made 1—and they'd hold that relationship through 9 swings to 3, 21 swings to 7, all the way to 30 swings to 10 and beyond; making and copying pages of typed zeros, totaling a million zeros posted along the school corridor walls—to see what a million is; watching the moon on successive twilights to see it from night to night approach and then pass Jupiter; noticing how many sheets of paper the light from a small flashlight bulb can be seen through; figuring out how to fit together the bones of a rabbit skeleton (a rabbit's pelvis bone, which is very elongated, looks more than anything like bones for the rabbit's ears); capturing some of one's own exhaled air in a tube and comparing it with air that a candle has burned in; watching a butterfly emerge.

None of the frameworks of the first week's discussion had engendered passion. But the work itself did. And soon I, a person with no science background, found myself captured, too. I was thrilled with what I was learning and how I saw myself learn. Here's a problem (see Figure 20–1) that I remember: If you have two bulbs attached to a battery as in circuit B, each is as bright as one bulb attached there as in circuit A. If the two bulbs are attached as in circuit C, they are both dimmer. My question was, how long will the batteries last? That is, how much "juice" is each setup using? My first prediction was that battery B will wear out twice as quickly as battery A, and batteries A and C will wear out at the same time. We set them up, with new batteries (and new bulbs, just to be sure) and went home for the night.

But I was rethinking this prediction at home in my living room that evening. I had worked enough with batteries and bulbs to know that something needed to run around from one end of the battery, through the bulb,

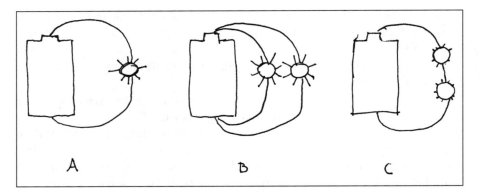

Figure 20–1

and connect again with the other end of the battery. I also knew that if a piece of wire made that connection, without a lightbulb along the way, the battery wore out *very* fast. I figured that the plain copper wire allowed it to run around more easily, and that the more it ran around, the more it got used up. (I was not at all clear about what the "it" was.) There needed to be a complete ring and in my experience it had usually been a ring of wire, though I had also made it work with aluminum foil, knives and forks, or a key chain. The idea came to me that the entire ocean of air in which the battery sat might also be able to make the link. It would no doubt take a *really* long time (since in my experience batteries that are sitting around in the air, unattached to anything, take months or years to wear out). But I had the sense that maybe air *could* carry this at a minuscule pace. And then the following idea came: Maybe there was a continuum between a piece of copper wire, which would allow whatever-it-was to be used up very quickly, and the ocean of air, which would allow it to be used up only *exceedingly* slowly.

As I imagined whatever-it-is-that-moves trying to run around from one end of the battery to the other, I saw that the bulbs in the B setup would help the top and bottom connect twice as well as the bulb in setup A, which supported my original prediction. But now I also saw that setup C would *keep* them from connecting so well—the little filament wires in the bulbs were not copper and they were very skinny, affording much less space for traveling through than the regular copper wire that was attaching the battery to the terminals of the bulb holder. Going through two little non-copper filament wires, one after the other, would be twice as much impediment as going through one—like going through a twice-as-long one-lane tunnel. In a sense, it would be a step on the continuum toward having only the ocean of air. So battery C should take longer to wear out than battery A. And this did prove to be the case.

I'll never forget the exhilaration of figuring that out. That feeling caught me, and kept me. And all that I learned there has stayed with me and taken me further. I have loved figuring out why a seesaw always rests with one end down, while the arm of a balance beam stays horizontal; knowing about using—and how *not* to use—booster cables; observing, as Robert Frost put it, that "Nature's first green is gold;" greeting the moon when I find it where I knew I would find it; appreciating the relationships between shadows on and reflections in a pond (also shadows on the bottom of the pond, which I found were distinct from shadows on the surface).

As David Hawkins (2002) pointed out, subject matter is in the world, it is not what is in books. The material that this curriculum presented, the material "presented from without," as Dewey puts it, was the world itself.

Over the years I have worked with people who were passionate about many different subject areas, who found ways to give learners of all ages various aspects of "the world"—the poem, the artifacts, the mathematical problem, the place to be mapped, the documents (see Duckworth 2001). Alythea McKinney (2004), for example, presented ninth and tenth graders with wooden butter molds, often-overlooked objects that helped nineteenth- and early twentieth-century farm women meet particular social and economic needs. As the students examined the objects, they called each other's attention to, and worked to make sense of, their sizes and shapes; their design, composition, style, and construction; their capacities and wear patterns. As they examined related documents and images from the same period, they observed users of the objects, their dress and their motions, and the arrangement and character of the spaces they and the objects inhabited. In thinking about and trying to integrate details like these—the kinds of evidence historians love—the students began to question their previous ideas about women of this time period, and to develop deeper, more complicated understandings of their lives.

All of these materials—from science, history, literature, mathematics, art, language—are able to invite learners' minds into dialogue with what teachers consider important to know about our world. The materials are filled with details that can captivate many different minds, as the world can! Lisa Schneier writes, "[It] is through the very complexities of a subject matter that its students gain access to it. The web of relationships that make up any real phenomenon provide its many entry points" (1995, 9). If materials are slim, the only questions likely to be posed are the teacher's. But if a question is not real for learners, minds are not brought to bear – the mind does not join the subject matter in a single reality. Lara Ramsey writes, "Without some recognition of why a problem is problematic—without a sense of contradiction or surprise—there is no foothold for approaching new understanding" (2002, 6). A problem is not a problem unless it is a problem; thought will not be given to it.

The questions the materials raise in learners, and the interest they provoke, must be seen as legitimate. *Nothing* happens until the interest has been touched. The reality of the subject matter of the world, and the reality of learners' minds—bringing them together is the reality that Dewey seeks. If the integrity of each is preserved, they cannot but meet.

We have found that one way to write curriculum is to write a case history. Here is what I did, here is what the learners noticed, here is what I did next, here is what happened this time alas, here is what I think I will do next time instead for these reasons—and so on.

We have also found that it is by no means always necessary to have highly developed curriculum materials. It is quite possible—and I would urge, essential—with what is at hand, and within a school system's required curriculum, to make a place where students find their own problems. Often at the basis of this work is the simple question, "What do you notice? The following are three examples.

Anne Collins, exasperated in her unsuccessful attempts to teach her seventh graders about mixed numbers, decided to do this: She wrote many mixed-number relationships all over the blackboard and asked the students what they noticed. They came up with everything they had not learned in her three previous lessons. "That strategy is one I use more and more in my teaching. I am constantly giving examples . . . and asking students what they notice, what can they say about the examples given, to write conjectures about what they are thinking" (personal communication, 2004).

Heidi Stewart was asked as a student teacher to teach about the use of commas; here is how she wrote about it:

> On Friday, I taught the lesson on commas that I had been working on. It went superbly well. The students were engaged in the lesson throughout the period and really seemed to both enjoy and learn the material (and we're talking about commas here). I also felt confident and knowledgeable about the purposes and pedagogy, especially after discussing my plans with [fellow students of teaching and learning].
>
> I introduced the lesson by asking if any of the students felt comfortable using commas. None did. I then spoke about the wonderful ideas I had seen in many of their papers and how important it was to polish their papers by using commas correctly, for, if they don't, their brilliant ideas will be lost in the world's judgment of their mechanics. I handed out the materials: sheets of comma-less sentences from the students' writing, sheets of correct comma usage in the students' writing for them to refer to, and newspaper clippings. After I had arranged the students to work in pairs, one student called me over. She wanted to tell me that I was "doing it

wrong," that I was supposed to give them all the rules regarding commas and then they were supposed to fill out the worksheets demonstrating what they had learned. (1995, 1–2)

After the pairs of students worked together on the passages that needed commas, the class as a whole worked on them with an overhead projection that allowed them to share a single conversation.

> When students disagreed on comma placement, much of the class would get involved in the debate. I would move the commas to different places on the transparency according to their thinking. During this time, the students were completely engaged in the class. Together we developed a few basic rules of comma usage. . . . I . . . was impressed with how much more engaged the students were when they had a chance to "figure things out." . . . One student came up after class and thanked me for the class, saying that she had always felt unsure of herself and her writing because of commas.

Lara Ramsey copied and distributed a two-page spread called "How the States Got Their Names" to discuss in her sixth-grade class. The question "What do you notice?" captivated the students and led to wide and deep insights into U.S. geography and history, including this remarkable one:

> I think I have a very important question. Oklahoma is named after Cho— how do you say it? Choctaw word for red people. What I'm wondering is, the Choctaw people were losing their land, and they wouldn't have been the ones to name a state without land. And if the people who made the land into a state were naming it, why would they use a Choctaw word if they were taking the land away from the Choctaws? It doesn't make any sense. (Ramsey 2002, 17)

This sixth grader's insight I think demonstrates that learners' minds, when engaged with real subject matter, necessarily bring us to its heart. And the heart of subject matter—unlikely as its surface may look—contains the "social aims, meanings, values" with which Dewey was centrally concerned in the quote that opens this chapter.

We bring students' minds to subject matter by offering it in all its complexity, allowing for attention to the specifics that can engage us, as the specifics of our living do.

21

Time, Trust, and Reflective Thinking in a Teacher Collaborative

LESLIE ALEXANDER

T he power in a classroom lies in the autonomy of teacher voice. In this time of No Child Left Behind (NCLB), where the work of a teacher is scripted and questions are predetermined, the role of the independent, spontaneous teacher is being eliminated. Teaching is often a solitary profession. Adults live in their classrooms with children, and regular colleague interaction rarely occurs. It is in these kinds of settings that teachers seem to lose their way and their ambition. Prepackaged curriculum leaves nothing for the thoughtful, intellectual teacher to pursue. Teaching is reduced to unwrapping the curriculum package and reciting the material. The importance of teacher voice and involvement in the creation of a small, public progressive school, therefore, may serve as a significant example for valuing teachers-as-thinkers.

The work of a group of teachers who took up the challenge of creating their own school is all the more striking set against the current trends in our profession. Here was a place where collaboration and thinking were valued and supported through the school's structure. The components of time, trust, and reflective thinking provided the underpinnings for the development of the collective. This grew out of a conscious choice by both families and staff to create a progressive, learner-centered school in a district where on a given day every fourth grader would be working on the same page, in the same book, at the same time, based on a pacing calendar provided by the district office. The district's methods, however, are currently the model for most public schools across America. It was within this context that the Muscota New School (MNS) opened its doors in 1992 and through its unique design came to be referred to as a "teacher collaborative."

MNS began as a five-classroom school on the fourth floor of a newly built elementary school situated on the banks of the Harlem River. Its name, Muscota, was derived from the Lenape tribe's word for "place of reeds" and actually described the place where the school was built. The Lenape were the Delaware tribe that once inhabited the northern end of Manhattan Island. This play on words, place of reeds/reads, was quickly adopted by a band of teachers and families who were committed to creating a learner-centered school in Washington Heights. Through work done with the Prospect Center, the school's founders understood the value of knowing children well; also the value of adults in the school knowing each other well through the examination of one another's work. Intervisitation, common planning times, and countless undocumented hours of being in one another's classrooms were central to the daily operation of the school and became the foundation for the collective that emerged.

Muscota was the dream of families living at the upper end of Manhattan who for years had been sending their children on long bus rides down into Central and East Harlem to the Central Park East schools. As a group these families were committed to progressive ideals. The pacing calendars and traditional methodologies of the local neighborhood schools forced them into enrolling their children in schools away from their community. A group of more than eighty-five diverse families, Inwood Designs in Education Association (IDEA), spent years laying the political groundwork needed to create the school, but it was the teachers who took the ideas and made them a reality.

This notion of a teacher collective was not something one could read about in 1992. It grew out of the professional needs of this small group to make a situation in which they could do their best work. In many organizations, lack of time and trust often prevent the development of nurturing collegial relationships. Not by design, but by practice, the MNS staff was able to overcome these common lacks. In looking back, there were some small things that were done that made an extraordinary difference.

The staff came together before Muscota's opening day and spent a week not only setting up inviting classrooms but also working directly with each other before the students walked through the doors. Open houses were held every afternoon for families to visit and bring things to donate to the classrooms. During that first planning week, the staff focused on curriculum topics and classroom design. Students were organized into multiage classrooms, and agreement was reached in terms of how these groupings would occur.

On the last day of the planning week the staff traveled to the Tiorati Environmental Center in Harriman State Park. This particular day was to be spent learning about one another. The task was to bring something of yourself to share with the group. That, in and of itself, was a risk-taking notion. At the time, none of the participants could have anticipated how vital this sharing was to be in the life of the school, but it became the foundation for what followed. During the morning session in the old stone Tiorati building, each staff member ventured out by sharing a poem, a piece of writing, a song that had personal importance. Some of the feelings revealed included the internal struggle of being biracial or coming to grips with the death of a parent. These glimpses into each person's reflective thinking would provide a touchstone for the collegial relationships that were to follow. Putting yourself out publicly in this way to strangers was evidence of the risk that was being taken by the collective group. This particular event, recalled often by the teachers, was characterized as momentous.

During the first months of the school's existence, it became customary for MNS staff members to get together every afternoon to go over the day's events. Processing, considering, and sharing became daily occurrences, helping to strengthen teacher relationships. These relationships in turn helped the staff make collective decisions in terms of curriculum, scheduling, and assessment.

Trust, as a critical characteristic of teaching, is rarely paid attention to in the lives of schools. However, trust is essential when teachers put their practice under the scrutiny of colleagues. Recently at the Six to Six Magnet School, another small, public progressive school in Bridgeport, Connecticut, there was a conversation about mathematics instruction and one staff member commented: "We have begun to trust one another, and that makes our conversations deeper and easier." These kinds of relationships were built through the structures that existed for the Muscota teachers. Seasonal retreats, Friday afternoon cultural gatherings, and trips together to the North Dakota Study Group provided space and opportunities that reinforced collegiality.

The structure of the school week provided for both business meetings and professional development meetings, along with the assessment/accountability work that took place at the end of each week. Families ran a clubs program for all the students each Friday afternoon, which helped build collaborative relationships between family and staff while providing invaluable time for teachers to work together.

The structure of each staff meeting provided additional forums for teachers to know each other in intimate ways. On a rotating basis, teachers would cover lunch and recess for the students. This provided a one-hour block of time during the day to deal with business items. Minutes of these meetings were recorded and shared. Collective decisions were made about the day-to-day workings of the school while more focused professional development conversations took place during the after-school meeting times.

Shared readings and reflections were a way to move beyond surface understandings to learn about each other's values and interpretive stances while also providing opportunities to discuss the literacy work of the school. This understanding helped when support was needed by individuals faced with difficulties regarding students and families. It led to trust and the trust, in turn, to deeper understanding. To hear a staff member say, "Wow, I never looked at it that way!" was evidence of the growth. The staff understood it was its collective responsibility to stay well informed and to share learning with others. Everyone had a voice and when those voices were heard, everyone grew. It exemplified a process that each person then brought to the classroom. Not only did teachers have voices but the children did as well.

Reflections became a regular feature of the professional development meetings using descriptive review techniques learned from the Prospect Institute. Through weekly reflections centered on words, we were able to create common ground and language—a way to come together around certain difficult topics. The staff learned to appreciate both the commonalities and differences among themselves. What was unusual was that the differences were embraced rather than criticized. Gaining the ability to say difficult things and to admit that one has something to learn became important elements of staff meetings. Collective vision with autonomous classroom practice became a fundamental principle of the school. The diversity in individual teaching practice was largely due to the nature of the collective.

This developing trust provided the underpinnings for teacher leadership. Recognizing one another's strengths both inside and outside of the classroom helped to ensure the smooth running of the school. Staff members took on different essential leadership roles. Each staff member, by her or his own determination, took the lead on a particular project that was either ad hoc or ongoing. Curriculum initiatives, assessment strategies, and daily scheduling became collective responsibilities with a point person in charge of each. Decisions were made on the direction we would take, initiatives to explore, topics for our staff meetings, and our priorities as a whole.

An example of this decision-making and collective responsibility played out in our investigation of narrative reports. From the beginning, the Muscota New School chose not to use the typical New York City report card to assess children's progress. Through the weekly meetings when children's work was described and archived, it was decided that only through narrative descriptions could the staff give families an adequate account of the students' progress. After the first year, these narrative reports became a topic of study. With the help of Cecelia Traugh, on behalf of the Prospect Institute, a question was raised: "Are the narrative reports actually serving the purposes for which they were intended?" This question was addressed through a series of descriptive reviews that looked closely at the teacher language used, at the commonalities or discrepancies that existed, and at the embedded values found in the reports. Through this process, a huge amount was revealed that helped the staff become more efficient and consistent at writing the reports. The willingness of staff members to open up their writing to close scrutiny was a testament to the relationships that had been built and the commitment to the collective.

As a group, the Muscota teachers traveled annually to the North Dakota Study Group. It was in this forum—"teacher panels"—that staff members could share their work. The NDSG provided a wider audience for teacher thinking, and in a progressive context, allowed the MNS staff to raise questions and to explore their thinking publicly. The yearly treks helped to affirm their practices and reinforced the teachers for the work they faced on a regular basis in the hostile territory of their local school districts. Muscota remained alive there amid the many who wanted them to fail. What was happening in this school was so vital but threatened the robotic practices seen in the rest of the district.

Public education is under threat. Federal legislation has a grip on the throats of teachers, silencing their voices and denying their need to think autonomously. The story of MNS helps us remember the true foundations of pedagogy—trust, reflection, and open, constructive relationships. These were the elements that helped sustain a small, progressive school during difficult times. The lessons learned are applicable to today's harsh educational environment and provide encouragement to those waging battles for teacher voices to be heard.

22

A Philadelphia Story

RHODA KANEVSKY, LYNNE STRIEB, AND BETSY WICE

Introduction

A group of teachers in Philadelphia has been meeting every Thursday afternoon since 1978. These meetings have provided a refuge, a source of renewal, and an intellectual meeting place for teachers from schools in the Philadelphia area—public schools and some independent schools—as we have struggled to hold onto our values about children and classrooms.

The Philadelphia School District

The School District of Philadelphia is strongly centralized, hierarchic, and monolithic. The Philadelphia Federation of Teachers, our labor union, is also centralized, hierarchic, and monolithic, echoing the organization of the school system. The School District ranks and orders schools from top to bottom and publishes the rank orders in newspapers. Children in the system are viewed through the lens of achievement according to test scores. Even charter schools (for which principals may choose staff independently) must give the achievement tests and their scores are also published. Teachers are often forced to focus on test preparation rather than encouraged to look closely at their children, to think about how they learn, to see their strengths, to enjoy their work on its own terms. Long before the No Child Left Behind (NCLB) legislation, the system tended to treat its teachers and students as anonymous, interchangeable parts. Teachers are seen as workers to be trained by outside experts and given curriculum kits from one publisher or another.

The Philadelphia Teachers' Learning Cooperative

The PTLC had its origins in the early 1970s at the Advisory Center for Open Education, a teachers' center in Philadelphia funded by the School District and the Follow Through program. Some of us went to the center every Thursday afternoon after school. We built furniture, made materials for our classrooms and attended workshops. We often remained at the center with brown-bag dinners to discuss classroom and educational policy issues. In 1972, the Advisory Center began its association with Patricia Carini and colleagues from the Prospect School in North Bennington, Vermont. Carini and teachers from Prospect were invited to speak at the center, and many of PTLC's founders attended seminars and summer institutes at Prospect. Those were the heady days of open education, the influence of British primary schools, and strong teacher support systems, when it looked as if the schools might actually become child-centered.

In 1978, when the Advisory Center lost its funding, we decided to meet anyway every Thursday, in participants' homes, to give ourselves a name, forego outside funding, and be independent of the School District. We also decided to continue our association with Prospect and to use the Descriptive Processes developed at the Prospect School. At first we had no idea whether PTLC would last past the initial six weeks, but more than twenty-five years later we still continue. Because of our independence, we have been able to focus on the things that are important to us, that matter to us as educators, paying attention to many of those things ignored in a test-driven environment. We've tried to live by democratic values as well as to talk about them as they are played out in our classrooms.

Two structures have enabled our group to stay alive and act on democratic values: the Prospect Descriptive Processes, used at each meeting, and the Weekly Schedule, created by the group at six- to eight-week intervals throughout the year.

The Prospect Descriptive Processes

Our weekly meetings follow formats developed at the Prospect School and Center. Prospect's Descriptive Processes gives these formats in detail, including: Descriptive Review of the Child, Descriptive Review of Children's Works, Reflection on a Keyword, Descriptive Review of Teaching as a "Work" and as an Art Form, Descriptive Review of an Issue, Recollection, and Descriptive Review of a School. (For an account of the formats, see Himley 2002, and Himley with Carini 2000.) The following characteristics are common to all the processes:

- Participants are seated in a circle so that they can see one another.
- Everyone has equal status, with no preference given to those with particular qualifications or positions.
- Participants speak in order. There is no "cross talk" during the time that the person is speaking or after she or he has finished.
- A presenter, if there is one, speaks uninterrupted until the presentation is complete.
- A chairperson summarizes, integrates, or pulls together at intervals, the main themes.
- A notetaker records the chair's summaries.
- Sessions usually end with implications stated for the classroom.

In the Descriptive Review of the Child, there is often a focusing question that directly elicits recommendations for the classroom—"How can Lisa get Jay to become more engaged in writing?" "How can Barbara support Carla's interest in her heritage?" Some Descriptive Reviews of children, and most Descriptive Reviews of work, have a less specific aim—"Charles is such a quiet member of the class. I want to see him more clearly." In the case of a Recollection, connections are made between our own experiences and our classroom experiences with children. When there is an issue under discussion, we talk about how what we've learned will make us think in new ways about our practice. We try to leave time at the end of each meeting to critique the process itself.

These established procedures mean that we start with a common understanding about how things will work at a PTLC meeting. Although no one feels obligated to come to every meeting, each person knows that when she or he does come it will be a safe place where everyone gets a turn and no one is interrupted. People who tend to be assertive find they must control themselves, that they cannot "take over" meetings. Those who are less assertive learn that their voices will also be heard. All perspectives are respected.

The Weekly Schedule

The schedule has helped us promote democratic values. The following is an example of the schedule for four weeks during the winter of 2003–2004:

February 19—Topic: Descriptive Review, second-grade child
February 26—Topic: Writing Workshop
March 4—Topic: Review of Practice
March 11—Topic: What I'm Saying; What They're Learning

The schedule also includes practical information about locations, starting and ending hours, and an invitation to "Come early for conversation and refreshments." The printed schedule is mailed out, posted on bulletin boards and various listservs, and passed informally from one person to another, often with the explanation that you don't have to be a member to come. Sometimes twenty or more people show up. Sometimes fewer than ten are there.

The schedules help to promote an activity that is inclusive and egalitarian. The participants determine the topics, chairs, presenters, and meeting places. At one scheduled meeting in March, for example, the group came together over supper to set up the next schedule to be distributed. On that evening, twelve of us showed up to hash out topics, chairs, presenters, and host homes for April, May, and June. The week before had been dedicated to Classroom Stories: Those who had come told about something going on in their teaching lives. Themes and issues that emerge from the Classroom Stories provide the raw material for the subsequent planning meeting. This procedure helps keep the group responsive to its members' interests and needs.

Here is an example of an evening of Classroom Stories that provided topics for other weeks:

- Lisa told about the difficulty of showing on the report card what her fifth graders actually understand in their reading.
- Christina talked about how bossy her student Pedro was becoming, how shrill her response felt to her.
- Gill raised questions about her students' writing.
- Susan, a school counselor, talked about legal issues that parents were raising around report cards.
- Amy told about the nonstop energy in her kindergarten (good and not so good).
- Erica told of the second-grade girl who had been crying lately, whose best friend moved away.

After we each told our story, the cochairs summarized the themes they had heard. The following week we crafted the January 8 to April 1 schedule.

The interest in teaching and evaluating reading led to Reflective Conversations on the word *comprehension* and on the topic of "partner reading." The interest in student writing and other expressive work led to meetings to talk about Writing Workshop, about independent work, about Amy's kindergartners' output, and also a session for sharing work that our students create as we and they respond to the district-imposed curriculum. We scheduled Descriptive Reviews of Practice to help two members think about their current and future classrooms and a Descriptive Review of one of Erica's students. We scheduled Reflective Conversations about report cards and civil rights issues in NCLB.

How the Meetings Influence Classroom Practice

When we get together for PTLC meetings, we put the chairs in a circle. We often find ourselves making the same arrangement in our classrooms. The circle of listeners fits our democratic processes. As we go around the circle, hearing one voice after another, each of us gains new perspectives on a question—whether our focus is the milkweed pod we are describing or a question about how a child might begin to read more easily. As adults, we come away from a Thursday meeting with different voices in our heads. Then we try the same approach in our classrooms so that we and the children can hear each others' voices and get to know each others' perspectives. Connie pushes her large teacher's desk off to the side so that she can watch the children more closely. Judy tries a circle with her English language learners and is amazed at how much more opportunity there is for each child to speak.

On Thursdays we adults become more active learners. In our classrooms our children become more active learners. Both in our Thursday group and in our classrooms, active learning helps us to see students more fully as individuals.

The Story of John

Looking back on years of participation, many of us can remember an occasion when we served as presenter and how it shifted our understanding of a particular child or of our whole classroom. Christina remembers what happened with John. It bothered her to hear other staff members talking about "that bad John," with insinuations about his family. She suspected she would get to see him in a different light if she brought some of his art for a Descriptive Review of Work. Christina had read *Caps for Sale* to the children and then asked them to draw something from the story. She saved John's picture to bring to the meeting where we were to do the review. Christina taped the picture to the wall, telling us only that John was seven and a student in the pre-first class. We began to describe the picture, taking turns pointing to certain shapes, colors, lines, and figures. In later rounds of comment, we mentioned whirly movement, solid figures, compressed energy. We thought of dancing and of spinning until you're so dizzy you fall. The chair reminded us of the places where we'd located energy: in the compression of the coils, on the tops of heads and the figures that made us think of bouncing puppets. Her restatement helped us look more closely at a line resembling an incomplete circle. We could almost sense the hand pushing the red marker swiftly out, to form the top of the circle, then swooping down and around and returning back in. "He goes way out, but he'll come back in," someone said.

We remarked how much the story seemed to be in the picture and what a powerful desire there was to get that story out. Christina eventually told us about the *Caps for Sale* assignment. We could begin to see hats, peddler, and monkeys (things that appear in the story). But what about the other figures? Christina told us what John had told her, that his uncle and mother had saved him from drowning in the swimming pool. He put that in the picture too.

In our final round, the time when group members comment about process, someone speculated that the *Caps for Sale* story got something else going. Christina said, "With John, people get caught up in saying 'Probably his mother. . . .' Today's discussion gave me a deeper appreciation of his story." Another person remarked about the sense we got "of a child's inner world, instead of spending our time jumping into psychoanalytic assumptions or generalizations about 'these parents,' or 'this environment'. . . ." From the power in that drawing, we learned a way to think about John as powerful —powerful emotionally and able to tell a story. Christina said what a different discussion we would have had if she had come to the group saying, "I'm worried about John's violence." Lynne recommended we continue our interest in John by scheduling a Descriptive Review of the Child. In March we did that review and were full of suggestions for helping John and others to see what John knew. At the end, Christina remarked, "I go to meetings of many groups that have as their goal promoting social justice. They talk about justice but these Thursday meetings are different." For us, the quest for justice grows out of a need to know who each of our students is.

Conclusion

John was Christina's student in 1999. Many Thursdays have come and gone since then. We have continued to meet to support each other and to keep alive a vision of education. PTLC has helped us hold onto what we value, seeing strengths in our students and in ourselves. The group helps us to maintain worthwhile child-centered practice in the face of an often hostile system, giving us courage to do what we believe matters.

PART SIX

Research and Evaluation

The issue of evaluation was the original impetus for the 1972 meeting at Grand Forks, North Dakota, which led to the formation of the North Dakota Study Group on Evaluation. Progressive views of research and evaluation are closely related, both relying primarily on close-up, qualitative methods.

Since his early work identifying the characteristics of "open education," Edward ("Ted") Chittenden has been consistent in his interest in the quality, rather than the quantity, of children's learning. In this chapter, questioning some of the usual assumptions, he discusses the delicate balance between teachers teaching and students learning in the light of his current research.

The perceived evils of standardized testing have come up many times in this book; Susan Harman gives an additional bite to the criticism in her description of her experiences as a progressive educator involved in an ongoing struggle against destructive testing practices in public education.

Patricia Carini gives a vivid example of a different way of looking—the Prospect Process of Review of Work—in which description takes precedence over judgment. A group of colleagues, looking together at a drawing by a five-year-old, gain in understanding and appreciation of both the work and its maker.

Finally, George Hein gives a broad overview of progressive evaluation theory, taking off from the educational writings of John Dewey. This chapter provides an appropriate finale to this work by and about the North Dakota Study Group on Evaluation (its original title). For progressive educators today, evaluation is at the heart of the matter: articulating, illustrating, and maintaining values is the aim, and constitutes the content, of this book.

23

What Is Taught, What Is Learned

EDWARD CHITTENDEN

The title of this chapter is from a paper I wrote many years ago, when I was just beginning to conduct research in schools. Although the contents of that paper seem thin to me now, I still like the title; it points to the ambiguous connection between teaching and learning.

To me, as a frequent visitor to schools and classrooms, teaching and learning stand in a Figure–Ground relationship. At times, teaching can be center stage, and much in the foreground, as teachers lecture, exhort, explain, demonstrate, ask questions. At such times, I get a sense of what the teacher believes important for the students and I may infer the purposes underlying the teacher's efforts. But there may be little indication, at least at that moment, of what this all means to students. Any evidence of their reactions is in the background, or perhaps even underground. They may ask a question or two, provide some answers, look interested, but as a visitor I have only hints of what it means to them. Nevertheless, like many classroom visitors, there is a tendency to be satisfied that if teaching is happening in such an overt manner, there must be corresponding learning.

At other times, especially in the early grades, the students' efforts to make sense come to the fore, while the teacher all but disappears or is on the periphery. I overhear children's conversations as they put something together or work on a project. The children's interests and the direction of their thinking are suggested by their comments, movement, or writing and drawing. But in these situations, as a visitor, I have little knowledge of the teaching history for what I observe. The scene is a snapshot; it does not reveal where the children were a few days, or months, previously, or how far they have come. On such occasions it can be difficult to *see* what the teacher has accomplished.

An anecdote from my friend Rhoda Kanevsky, who taught first grade in Philadelphia for many years, speaks to my point about the visibility of teaching. She once told me that her new principal (one in a series of principals) had announced her plan to visit each classroom to get to know the staff, as teachers—a good idea, Rhoda felt. The principal chanced to visit Rhoda's classroom during journal writing time when the children, more or less independently, were making entries in their booklets while Rhoda gave help to individuals. The principal remarked that she enjoyed the visit, but would need to return at a later point when Rhoda was "teaching."

Taking my thoughts about this one step further, it must be daunting to be a student teacher in settings such as Rhoda's. The teaching side of the story is not always apparent. It must take a while, as it has taken me, to look beyond or behind the children's work for the teacher's work.

I have sometimes reprimanded teacher friends for telling only half the story when giving an account of their students' accomplishments. Their presentation of the children's drawings, writings, and language—so rich in detail—offers too few cues of how such achievement was supported. A close look at children's work can be at the heart of professional learning, but the "outsider" viewing the same work may come away with the conclusion that the children are wonderful. I ask myself, "When evidence of learning is in the foreground, do we (visitors) necessarily conclude there must be teaching?"

The trajectory of my research experience with teachers over the years reflects the challenge of moving beyond dimensional perceptions of classroom life. In the 1970s teaching and learning were sometimes portrayed as competing for space. Simply put, either you directly teach children what they are supposed to learn, or you let them figure it out by themselves. Such a relationship was embodied in the evaluation framework used by the Office of Education (OE) to assess the success of the different educational "models" being supported by Project Follow Through (kindergarten and primary grades). The models were arrayed on a continuum from teacher-centered at one end to child-centered at the other, with various points in between. The OE's evaluation plan called for administering achievement tests to children across the various models to determine which was most successful. Described as "a horse race" by one of the program officers, the plan provoked much opposition, especially from the child-centered wing. The use of tests was certainly a central issue, but equally problematic was categorical representation of classrooms.

In this context, our Early Education Group at the Educational Testing Service (ETS) took on an exploratory project for the Office of Education. (In addition to me, the group's members were Marianne Amarel, Anne Bussis, Rosalea Courtney, and Masako Tanaka.) We were asked to look closely at one of the models, Education Development Center (EDC), to formulate assessment strategies that address some of the objections. This led to a one-year collaboration involving our group at ETS and the advisory group at EDC, a relationship that eventually linked us to many educators who were active in the early days of the North Dakota Study Group.

During the project we visited EDC Follow Through sites across the country, and interviewed teachers and administrators, as well as EDC staff. Teachers in these settings were moving away from conventional basal programs to more "open" formulations of curriculum, allowing greater responsiveness to children's interests. It soon became apparent, from our visits, that the Office's evaluation scheme based on a continuum of "centeredness" made little sense. Classrooms with robust evidence of individual children's accomplishments (child-centered) were at the same time settings that reflected significant, decision-making responsibilities by teachers (teacher-centered)—whether such decisions pertained to establishing the classroom setting, providing guidance and instruction, or revising curriculum.

One of our first recommendations to OE was to replace the horse-race continuum with something more complex, reflecting the complexity of early education reform. As starters, we proposed a two-dimensional framework that allowed initiative from children to coexist with initiative from teachers (Bussis and Chittenden 1970). At a minimum, this would underscore the progressive view that teachers learn while children learn, and would distinguish the "open" classrooms, envisioned by EDC, from caricatures of child-centeredness that presumed permissiveness and minimal adult direction.

Educators told us that our report to the Office of Education helped them clarify their own positions when dealing with assessment issues. I do not believe, however, that our recommendations had any effect on national evaluation plans. But the project did serve as a starting point for subsequent school-based studies.

Thinking back on decades of studies, I believe we initially aspired to document the connection, if you will, between what is taught and what is learned. But in reality, the trajectory of our research zigged and zagged from one to the other. At times teaching, or more broadly, professional development was a focus. At other times, children's learning captured attention.

In the 1980s, the ambitious longitudinal study of beginning readers, which brought us together with many educators in the North Dakota network, yielded ample classroom-based records of the different ways that children learn to make sense of print and to find meaning in reading. The study was designed in collaboration with teachers; therefore, much of the documentation was derived from teachers' observations of their students. Yet in the final report (Bussis et al. 1985), these teachers are in the background, while patterns in the records of their children take the foreground. Critics pointed out that only by implication does the study shed light on instructional methods—a criticism parallel to my own "complaints" when teachers present their students' work.

In subsequent years, working with some of the same teachers, we examined children's ideas about the natural world, particularly as revealed in classroom conversations (Chittenden 1990). This resulted in a great many records of children's talk, about bugs they encountered, about shadows and light, or about what happens to the sun at night. In these records, we can certainly see general connections between what was offered in the classroom and the children's remarks; that is, children who had observed metamorphosis of monarchs had much to say on the subject. But nature let loose in the classroom invites memory, observation, and speculation. The details of children's observations, ideas, and questions took directions (and misdirections) that went well beyond what the teachers expected or thought they had "taught."

Currently, I am an advisor to the Science and Nature Program for Young Children within the American Museum of Natural History. If there is merit in the idea of direct instruction, it is exemplified by the millipedes in that program. I watch as the four-year-olds closely observe the creatures, which have been removed from their classroom habitat of leaf litter and placed on a rug. They are "giant" tropical millipedes, some seven or eight inches in length. Their movements seem deliberate as they investigate their surroundings. The children, from a nearby Head Start program, are weekly visitors to the Museums's program and so have experience with careful observation of animals in this setting.

Clearly, the children are intrigued; some are more cautious about holding the animals in order to feel their many legs in action, but all are observant. They note that when the animals crawl on your hand, they "tickle" or "stick" like a piece of creeping Velcro. As I watch with the Figure–Ground image in mind, it strikes me that the millipedes have taken the foreground as teachers. The classroom teacher artfully stepped aside so that the animals, in their myriapodal ways, could give the children firsthand lessons in fundamentals of the natural world—that each creature has particular ways of moving and has definite preferences for places to live and be. You may want it to run, or hop, or eat something else, but it stays with its own rules; and if you watch, you begin to realize there are such rules. You begin to view the animal as a living thing, like you, but with different requirements. (It is no accident that children will put "smiley faces" on their otherwise anatomically appropriate drawings of the animals.) To become curious about such rules is a first step of scientific inquiry.

Observing children observing animals over the weeks, reminds me of David Hawkins' view (1966) that significant concepts in science are "unteachable" in the conventional sense. A word or a name for a concept can be taught, but important ideas are acquired across cumulating encounters and given shape by the individual.

In the American Museum program, as in the classrooms in our studies of reading and science, there is a "back-and-forthness"—as Lillian Weber might say—among teacher, children, and the stuff of learning. A child's understanding and appreciation for the diversity of living things evolves over time rather than via a lesson or two. Similarly, children's powers as readers are acquired along different routes, within the same classroom, as they come to know the regularities of print and the rhythms of literature. And the more complex the stuff, the greater the challenge to see connections between what is taught and what is learned.

24

Confessions of a Test-Resister

SUSAN HARMAN

In 1962, Banesh Hoffmann wrote the *Tyranny of Testing*, the first serious critique of testing. That was the year I graduated from college, and my career has been haunted by the tests, up to and including today, as my charter school lives under the guillotine of the federal law cynically named No Child Left Behind (NCLB). If the test scores of my school's very poor children don't constantly improve, the Title I money we use to broaden our kids' cultural capital (through art and music classes and trips to concerts, museums, farms, and scientific natural wonders) will be taken from us and diverted to after-school tutoring by for-profit companies, busing kids to higher-scoring schools, or converting our charter school into a *charter* school.

This last sanction is my personal favorite because it's a great example of this law's carelessness since, in the case of existing charters, it makes no sense. What I think it really means is that our failing school will be usurped by a for-profit brand-name charter company, or EMO (Education Management Organization). The federal law is so single-mindedly focused on privatizing education that some of us call it "No Corporation Left Behind." As if NCLB were not bad enough, the president of the California School Board pushed through a law that says charters whose scores aren't high enough will be closed.

In 1962, I didn't know I was going to be a teacher. My first career was in politics. I was working in the New York City Mayor's Office in 1970, helping to organize the first women's march in honor of the fiftieth anniversary celebration of women's suffrage. The Civil Rights Movement, the New Left, and the Women's Movement had filled me with a sense of power and possibility. That same year I read Joseph Featherstone's *New Republic* articles (1967) about British primary education, and heard about Lillian Weber's work in

New York City's Harlem (both became members of the soon-to-be North Dakota Study Group). I decided to stop trying to change the world from the top and to start organizing from the bottom up. After a long conversation with Weber, I registered for her City College of New York progam—The Child and the Individualized Curriculum.

I student taught in one of Weber's Open Corridor schools in Harlem where Deborah Meier (another Study Group member) was the advisor. Then, in 1972, Weber started the Workshop Center for Open Education at City College. It was the year I graduated from her master's program and the same year the North Dakota Study Group first met. These two institutions have complemented and supported each other all these years. The Workshop Center provided for those of us in New York City the kind of collegial camaraderie and reassurance that the Study Group provides in a more diffuse way for those of us scattered throughout the rest of the country. Their histories are woven together for many of us who contributed to this book.

My first teaching job was as the reading teacher in the same Harlem school where I had student taught. I myself had been one of those kids who read cereal boxes. As an adult, I read constantly and compulsively, panicking if I didn't have a book in my bag for fear that I might have a few minutes between meetings with nothing to read. The moments I love best in teaching are when the child I'm reading with comes to a word she doesn't know and says urgently, "Don't tell me!" In that moment I see her curiosity and excitement in solving the puzzle, her drive to understand, and her confidence that she can do it. It's thrilling.

So it is particularly difficult for me—as both a reader and a reading teacher—to watch the tests mismeasure that experience and corrupt it by turning school into test prep. The tests and the standards and the packaged, teacher-proof programs focused on raising test scores assume all children are the same—interchangeable parts on an educational assembly line. But Weber taught me to individualize the curriculum to meet each child's interests and needs. The "standardistos" (Susan Ohanian's term) don't know and don't care about the individual child. Children are resisting the effort to homogenize them by dropping out of school in shocking numbers.

I went back to graduate school and got my doctorate in special education and school psychology, supporting myself by teaching at Lesley College with George Hein and Brenda Engel (both Study Group members). Sometime in the late 1970s Eleanor Duckworth was Lesley's graduation speaker, and "the having of wonderful ideas," the title of her well-known book (1996), became part of my vocabulary and part of my definition of a good school—a place where children and adults are frequently having wonderful ideas. In her speech she talked about looking at, and seeing, children in contrast to the tests, standards, and programs, which are blind.

In graduate school, my assessment professor told us to "Remember that a test is just a structured observation." That permanently demystified tests for me, and has helped me remain irreverent toward them ever since. I know too much about how they're constructed, have given thousands to children I know very well, and see how little they can tell me about children. In fact, it's what I know already about the children that helps to explain their scores, not the other way around. The testers assume that the scores tell us things we don't already know about children ("Maria needs work on suffixes"), but in my experience it's we teachers who have to explain to the bureaucrats why that class scored low. For example, their teacher got pregnant and they had five substitutes that year; or a pair of twins came from the mountains of Guatemala, hadn't been to school, and couldn't read in Spanish, much less in English.

In the end, the tests are stunningly uninformative. Taking a cue from Deborah Meier's *Reading Failure and the Tests* (1973), I have often asked a child why he chose the answer he did. He has almost always been able to read both the passage and the question and had a good reason for his answer, which, however, wasn't necessarily what the test-makers decreed as correct. So his score made it look as though he couldn't read when in fact, because of differences in class, linguistic usage, background knowledge, or maybe just quirkiness, he disagreed with the test-maker about which answer was right. These experiments give me a lot of information about the child (his literacy, his cultural capital, his take on the world), and a lot also about the test-makers (their biases, their ignorance of child development, and their dearth of experience with young children). But these wrong answers *don't* tell me the child can't read, his teacher can't teach, or his school is failing.

A ten-year-old expert reader once told me, "Of course I don't read the tests the way I read anything else. I don't read *Harry Potter* wondering what I'm going to be quizzed on. I read it because I want to find out who'll win at quidditch." If the tests are a unique genre of reading, as this sophisticated child knew, then what they tell us—the score—is restricted to that genre, and is irrelevant to all the other kinds of reading. That is, the tests tell us how good a test-taker the child is, not how good a reader she is.

Testing is a much bigger business now than when Hoffmann wrote about the "business of testing" and identified the "big five" test publishers: Harcourt, Brace & World (now Harcourt), the Psychological Corporation (now part of Harcourt), California Test Bureau (now CTB/McGraw-Hill), SRA (now part of CTB/McGraw-Hill), and the Educational Testing Service (still ETS). There was a near-monopoly of test-makers then, but the use of their products—tests and textbooks—wasn't mandated as it effectively is now by the federal government and its funding regulations. Schools, districts, and states could choose whether or not, and with what, to test.

Now if they don't choose the tests and the scripted programs "recommended" by the cabal of "scientists" that runs the show, they don't get Title I money.

In 1978, I became the psychologist at Central Park East (CPE) in New York City. Many of the teachers there had worked with Patricia Carini (Study Group member) on the Descriptive Review of the Child. This approach builds the picture of a child through careful collection of her work over time and observations of her made by several adults. Carini's work prepared me for the Learning Record, my school's evaluation tool.

The Learning Record (LR) is a comprehensive portfolio system that includes interviews, observations, miscue analyses, running records, and work samples. The LR originated in England, but came to California via the Study Group. Mary Barr, the director of the California Literature Project, came to an annual meeting and was given, hot off the press, a copy of the *Primary Language Record* (Barrs et al. 1988). Barr recognized immediately that it was the assessment scheme she had been looking for and adapted it as the California Learning Record (Barr et al. 1999).

At my school, we use the LR because it is consistent with progressive pedagogy; it is personal, humane, thoughtful, developmentally appropriate, ongoing, learner-centered, empathic, and useful. Unlike the tests, it includes a procedure for ensuring reliability. A sample of each teacher's evaluations is checked against her documentation by other teachers in her school and by a national group of experienced teachers. In this way, we get the teacher's in-depth subjective knowledge of a child, as well as reliability.

In the early eighties, the tests were gathering steam to roll over progressive approaches to teaching and learning. New York City began flunking third graders who didn't pass the tests, as it did again this past year when it flunked 5,000 third graders. I decided I could be more useful to the progressive movement by devoting myself to fighting the tests, so I left CPE and went to work with FairTest, a public advocacy group devoted to identifying and promoting equitable, reasonable school assessment procedures.

I'm still working with FairTest in my spare time, organizing the Resistance in California, and the tests are still tyrannizing education. Under No Child Left Behind, their hegemony has become nearly absolute. Test scores have replaced all other ways of describing learning and achievement. Teacher and principal evaluations are based on test scores, schools are rewarded or punished based on test scores, real estate agents advertise houses based on local test scores, and even custody suits have been settled based on which parent's neighborhood school has higher test scores. Our infatuation with tests has become a toxic obsession.

Throughout its history of more than thirty years, the North Dakota Study Group has both critiqued the testing industry and explored authentic ways of evaluating children's progress. In 1978, the Study Group supported Diana Pullin in her landmark lawsuit (Debra P. v. Turlington) establishing the necessity of opportunity to learn. The NDSG, under its own imprint, published four monographs critiquing standardized testing and twelve describing authentic methods (see listing of monographs at the back of this book).

Vito Perrone, the original convener and leader of the NDSG, coordinated *Testing and Evaluation: New Views* (Perrone and Cohen 1975) for the Association for Childhood Education International and edited *Expanding Student Assessment* (1991b) for the Association for Supervision and Curriculum Development.

The critiques and the alternatives overlap; in each of the presentations of authentic evaluation is an implicit critique of the narrow, competitive, discriminatory, and useless tests. If one connects the dots that are the titles of these monographs, the picture that emerges is of the commitment to carefully make each individual child visible and known, because it is only then that she or he can be reached and taught. In my work as a teacher, psychologist, writer, principal, and organizer, I continue to try to live out this commitment to care about the children in our care. I rely on the NDSG's annual meeting to hear real-live examples of colleagues doing the thinking and the work that actualizes progressive principles. I squirrel away stories and take home papers with which to inspire my staff. Increasingly, I depend on the stalwart friendship and moral integrity of the North Dakota Study Group.

25

Prospect's Documentary Processes
Learning to See/Learning to Describe

PATRICIA F. CARINI

The scene is the 2002 meeting of the North Dakota Study Group on Evaluation. I had been asked to present a paper that, among other things, would set the stage for a description of a children's artworks session, which was to immediately follow the plenary session. I decided to do the stage-setting with the help of a drawing and, more specifically, with the story of describing that drawing. It was, as I said on that occasion, a story constructed to show the working side of the discipline of looking and describing at the heart of Prospect's documentary processes. In the talk, I capsulized that discipline, as I have many times before, with a succinct and well-turned sentence from social philosopher Raymond Williams: "We learn to see a thing by learning to describe it" (1961, 23).

I might have added that learning to describe as it is practiced at Prospect is to unlearn habituated perceptions and to disrupt automatic judgmental, evaluative responses. I might have also gone the next step to say that by breaking free of habituated perceptions of a child, a classroom, an activity, or any subject, I or you or any of us is freed to act toward that subject with a newfound responsiveness and fullness. To say that in slightly other words, by telling the story of describing the drawing, I am making the case for an equation between new ways of seeing and new ways of acting—the one directly leading to the other. In this sense (and some others), it is a story that enacts the *continuity* between beholder and beheld, and the reciprocal, life-affirming benefits of that continuousness.

I present the drawing (see Figure 25–1), as I did at the NDSG meeting, with only slight context. It was made in 1975. The child who drew it was then five and attending Prospect School in North Bennington, Vermont. I will

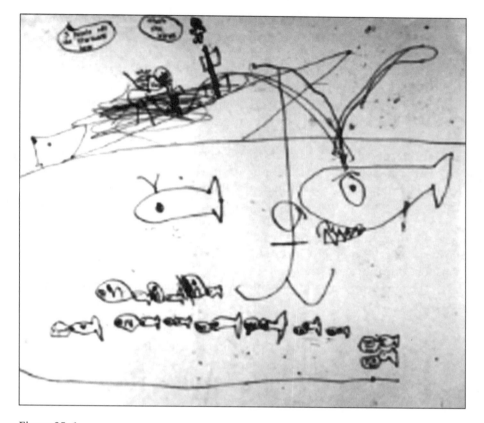

Figure 25–1

call him Mick, not his actual name. His collection of works, with permission from his family, was published in the *Reference Edition of the Prospect Archive* (1985), along with those of thirty-five other children.

The story begins in the summer of 2000 at Prospect's annual Summer Institute. Five of us, all close colleagues and longtime associates, were launching a long-term project to explore what, apart from historical interest, Prospect's collections of children's works continued to offer, and how the collections might be made more accessible to other educators and students of childhood. Besides me, the assembled group included Beth Alberty, Peg Howes, Rhoda Kanevsky, and Alice Seletsky. It was in the context of that project that we spent an hour or so describing Mick's drawing.

Because I was the one among us who at that point was the most familiar with Mick's works, I made the selection. With some difficulty, especially because this collection is extraordinarily large (2,500 pieces made from age five to age twelve), I narrowed the choice to two. One drawing, "the kickballer" (as Mick named it), with its sharply angled arms and legs, attracted me for its economy of line and vigor of expression and because the kickballer is a common presence in Mick's work at ages five and six. My other choice, and the one I settled on, is this drawing of a ship. Ships also recur, and indeed, persist across the eight years the collection spans. The deciding factor, though, was the dimension of the drawing. Drawings on this large a scale, or larger, dominate Mick's collection up to his ninth year.

How I am going to tell this story of the discipline of learning to see and describe by practicing it is through a sampling of our descriptions as we sat that summer afternoon with Mick's drawing in the center of our circle. When I have given the flavor of how we did that descriptive work, I will collapse the story to connect what it tells with broader implications of what at Prospect we call "another way of looking," and the import of those implications for educating and schools.

I begin with a selection of the comments made in the first round of description.

- *First describer*—It is a large drawing, and except for some tiny filled-in figures on top of what appears to be the deck of a ship, it is a line drawing done in red marker.
- *Second describer*—The ship dominates the top of the page but takes up less space than the fish below.
- *Third describer*—There is a harpoon-like piece of equipment, in action to judge by the unfurling line. That and the presence of whalelike fishes (they have spouts) suggest the ship is a whaler.
- *Fourth describer*—That it's a whaler seems confirmed by the words spoken by the figures on the deck. The sailor figure leaping or suspended in midair says, "There she blows!" The figure at the tiller responds, "Where does she blow?" The midair sailor calls back, "Three points off the bow."

From this first naming of elements in the drawing, the descriptions expanded. The ship, we noticed, is entering from the left. We see only the prow, which is drawn as an extended triangle, with the implication that both sea and ship continue beyond the boundary of the page. The next describer wondered for a minute about a puzzling shape drawn at the back of the prow, and then went on to observe how the sense of a ship in motion is accentuated by a curved horizon line over which the prow appears to rise.

Another of us moved on to the fish, noting they are numerous. Of the two that seem to be whales, she observed that the bigger of these is sort of tubby in the middle, with the teeth kind of hanging out there. "A sperm whale," someone responded.

The continuing description included these comments: The bigger of what appear to be whales also has a very large eye, with what seems to be an eyebrow, and because of the positioning of the eye, it appears to be looking out at us, the viewers. What appears to be the anchor line visually blocks the movement of the larger whale. That and facial expression, give an impression that the larger whale is stuck—not able to get away. The smaller whale, though not literally blocked, is very still.

Descending a level, the smaller fish claimed our attention and made us laugh. They are so many and so humorous and certainly not still or silent. The front fish are saying "Yipers!" (written in an adult's hand, apparently dictated). Others are saying "No" (in a child's hand) with the "N" coming out of the mouth first as it does when speaking. The last two little fish bringing up the rear are calling, "Wait for me." For the flotilla of fish the exit to the left is unimpeded, and it seems apparent that they are getting out of the action as quickly as possible.

As we traveled further into the drawing, compositional features began to fall together. Among the things we noticed was the depiction of multiple layers of action: men in interaction with each other and whales; whales and their fate impacting on fish. To complicate that, the action happens from three directions: the ship entering from the left and angled to the right; the whales oriented left but seemingly stationary at mid-level; the fish flotilla in the bottom plane, exiting to the left. Some of the action is vocal.

We wondered if more than one perspective is represented. Taken from the angle that whales blow on the surface, the bottom line can be read as shore. Looked at as a cross section, the bottom line suggests some further depth or the bed of the sea. Both perspectives work, so it leaves some ambiguity—but without disturbing the coherence of the drawing. The picture is also like a cutaway, a cross section, a map.

Sampling now from another part of the description, we noticed that though the artist is depicting a large, full-scale narrative, it is also economical. The drawing, we thought, has order and solidity even though energy abounds in flurries of line, the buoyancy of the anchorlike object, the sailor suspended midair. We observed that there is a lot of knowledge propelling this drawing: of ships, of whales, of whaling, of how fish travel in schools, of how a story works. A drama is played out before our eyes: Will the whale be caught? Will the fish escape?

To our delight, we realized that we also could see the child's hand at work. The pause points in the red whale outlines that leave a "dot" suggest that Mick has a practiced way of making fish. It seems he may start in the middle or point of the tail fin—a beginning place that allows him to proceed from there in either direction to construct the fin and then move on smoothly to the body. One of us suggested the ship prow also had a "learned" or practiced look, as if Mick has figured out a way to do ships.

There was more, yet even a small sampling yields a lot. As the session (lasting about an hour) drew toward its close, I added in pieces of what I had learned from the larger collection. I showed the reverse side of the ship drawing, which strongly suggests a first try, a practice try, that led to another try—the drawing we described. I told how I noticed that at ages five and six, Mick more typically uses the second side of the paper to continue the action begun on the first. One of us pointed out that by that means he doubles the already large space available for his creation. I added that on some occasions he had an adult write a caption for each side, typically with this message: "This is the end of the first side of the picture," and on the reverse, "This is the end of the whole story."

On other occasions, I showed arrays of Mick's visual artworks to show some of the spanning themes, motifs, and mediums in the collection as a whole. To give some flavor of these, I showed a selection of artworks, including a sampling of the kickballers—so notable for the energy of the line; several Viking drawings, as examples of the recurrence of human figures in action across the collection; other depictions of ships, also recurrent across the collection and illustrative of Mick's experimentation and practice of form; and some paintings, striking for their lyricism, made at age twelve.

At the NDSG meeting, following this sampling of the collection, I returned to the story of learning to see the ship drawing by describing it. I told that when we had concluded the description, even though the day had been long and our meeting space was cramped, we dawdled and prolonged the conversation. It was a lingering I have noticed on many other occasions. There were more chuckles over the fish and the addition of small points. There was marveling at the complexity of the picture with its several layers of action. We couldn't quite tear ourselves away from the drawing for by then, you see, we were a little in love with it—or maybe a lot in love with it.

And the child, the maker? Well, how could we resist him? How could we not appreciate a child who thinks so big, with such an expansiveness and activeness about him? How could we not wonder what would happen to that bigness without space sufficient to express it? How could we not notice all he brings to learning? How much knowledge he has soaked up by age five and how much he seems to have taught himself by practicing? How could we not ponder the educational implications of his attentiveness to form, in drawing and in dialogue, and want to explore further how expressiveness in line and gesture is connected to an equal liveliness of language? We were enticed, intrigued—looking forward to getting to know him better. He was the apple of our eye.

So I think I understand the dawdling. By the small act of joining the drawing on its own terms, content to be alongside it for a mere hour or so, to not judge or score it, or theorize about it, it returned so much. From the simple act of noticing and appreciating, the drawing sprang to life, and the drawer along with it. That is surely sufficient, and yet there was more. The drawing, so particular, so specifically the handiwork of this child, not thinkable or makeable by any other, worked the peculiar magic of the particular when given undivided attention, to vault beyond itself, to open a vaster space. And carrying us with it, to shine a small, bright light on the wonder of the human imagination, the capacity in each child and every child, and in us all, to make and remake the world.

Anthony + the yellow

26

A Progressive Education Perspective
on Evaluation

GEORGE E. HEIN

Rewards and high marks are at best artificial aims to strive for; they accustom children to expect to get something besides the value of the product for work they do. The extent to which schools are compelled to rely upon these motives shows how dependent they are upon motives which are foreign to truly moral activity (1915, 297).

—JOHN AND EVELYN DEWEY
SCHOOLS OF TOMORROW

This chapter presents a broad overview of evaluation based on John Dewey's educational theory and practice. Dewey's writings represent the most detailed and fundamental articulation of progressive education available. He considers evaluation, as he does all educational issues, within the broader context of social and moral philosophy. For Dewey, evaluation that relies on extrinsic rewards for something that should have intrinsic value not only diminishes its worth as an educational goal but it also obscures the moral implications of any evaluation policy.

Progressive educators, like all educators, struggle with the difficult task of evaluation. No educational system is complete without judgments, but decisions about people and programs are always difficult. There are three main areas where evaluation is significant and judgments are needed: student progress with all the surrounding intense political and moral issues; teacher evaluation; and evaluation of educational programs, ranging from the effectiveness of specific curricula or pedagogic methods to judgments about schools and school systems.

what's it for?
micro
macro

Each level of evaluation—student, teacher, and program—needs to take into account the entire context of schooling. Evaluation should not be a separate "technical" issue, conceptualized, analyzed, and implemented independently from the entire educational setting. Before considering the three levels, I will describe Dewey's views on the broad context of evaluation: the moral purpose of education, uncertainty and change, and the individual and society.

The Primacy of the Moral Purpose of Education

A holistic conception of evaluation as an integral part of education goes back directly to John Dewey's formulation of progressive education as a moral enterprise to support a democratic society. For him, all aspects of schooling had to meet a moral standard: Would they contribute to building a progressive society?—one that "endeavor[s] to shape the experiences of the young so that instead of reproducing current habits, better habits shall be formed, and thus the future adult society be an improvement on their own" (Dewey 1944/1916, 79). For Dewey, such an improvement was a democracy in which all members had the opportunity to participate fully in social and economic life, and every individual able to fully realize his or her potential within a socially interactive community. Dewey was never naïve on this subject. He realized that the full achievement of his vision was unlikely, but he conceived a society that progressed from its condition then (as now) of extreme economic differences (in his words, making some members virtually economic "slaves"), intolerance toward immigrants and other minority groups, and serious lack of opportunities for many to better their conditions or participate fully in the society. Applying this moral criterion to educational evaluation clarifies why most current school practices fail to meet the needs of children, schools, and society.

Uncertainty and Change

Besides moral concerns, there are other aspects of Dewey's overarching worldview that should inform any discussion of evaluation. Perhaps nothing is as important in articulating a progressive stance on evaluation as Dewey's concept that the world is an uncertain place, that actions need to be guided by and respect actual experience—the human condition in constant flux—and that the nature of any human enterprise needs to be examined continually and modified to respond to the consequences of previous decisions and actions. This theme of uncertainty and change, which is so difficult for us to accept in our own lives despite overwhelming evidence, cannot be overstated.

For Dewey, life's problems were never "solved," but part of a continuing progress toward better conditions that lead to new problems to be addressed. As a result, evaluation concepts, methods, and practices need to be constantly rethought and reconsidered.

This particular aspect of progressive evaluation challenges a number of current practices. For example, the search for fixed standards for curriculum, testing, promotion, and so on are all suspect to the extent that they claim to be absolute and immutable. In practice, the realities of school systems (and wider politics) lead to shifting standards along with modifications in testing and program goals. These changes, however, are usually viewed as corrections of errors or unfortunate necessities based on political considerations, rather than as a necessary component of an ongoing search for useful practices.

The Individual and Society

A third concern for Dewey in regard to evaluation is "the problem of the relation between individual freedom and collective well-being" (Mayhew and Edwards 1936/1965, xiii), a theme Dewey still considered "urgent and acute" forty years after he began his Laboratory School (as it still is today). Schools need to value and to encourage individual development and to support children's growth into independent thinkers who can question ideas and make informed decisions. At the same time, they have the responsibility to develop cooperative, socially productive practices that will allow democracy to flourish. The goal for students is to "learn to *act* with and for others, while you learn to *think* and to judge for yourself" (Dewey 1931, 98). Evaluation at every level needs to address this tension.

The exclusive use of standardized, norm-referenced tests, mostly paper-and-pencil (or some modern technological version of these) to make "high-stakes" decisions about children, teachers, and programs, hardly meets basic criteria for supporting progress toward a democratic society where all individuals are valued and provided with an education that develops their capacities to be thinking, inquiring members of a collaborative society. It ignores the needs at both ends of this tension, encouraging neither individual development nor supporting cooperative action.

Student Evaluation and Standardized Testing

Comparing students with each other leads to the inevitable categorization of some as scoring "better" and some as scoring "worse"—judgments that get generalized to the children themselves. Many of the negative psychological aspects of schooling come from the constant comparative judgments made

in such assessment atmospheres rather than recognizing the unique qualities of each child and his or her progress and development. That this type
of categorization contradicts what we know about child development has
been stated often. But from a progressive education perspective, the criticism is deeper; that is, such judgments do not assist children to develop
into responsible, thinking, and cooperating citizens and are counterpro-
ductive to developing a participatory democracy.

Tests that are separate from assessments embedded within the curriculum, and especially high-stakes tests, substitute external rewards for intrinsic
satisfaction derived from learning. "This assumption that education is not
natural and attractive—inherently so—reacts most disastrously upon the
responsibility of both the teacher and the child." (Dewey 1906, 242) When
the reward (or punishment) from an educational experience comes from the
grade or test outcome and not from the completion of the task, then the goal
of education is shifted from reflecting on the entire experience and its possibility of further education to pleasing the teacher (or the employer).

The complex statistical superstructure that often hides the actual results of student testing, compounded by the secrecy associated with high-
stakes academic tests, has been criticized for obscuring technical weaknesses
of tests and making it difficult to catch inevitable scoring errors and misin-
terpretation. In addition to serious questions about the technical validity of
standardized tests, the tests measure a narrow range of skills and concepts;
contribute little to providing teachers with formative assessment of student
strengths and weaknesses; break knowledge down into separate, uncon-
nected fragments; and assume that students, classes, and schools can be rank-
ordered on simplistic scales regardless of the myriad factors that influence
the results. In fact, economic variables can account for roughly four-fifths of
the variance between individual students, classes, and schools. Standardized
tests measure parental socioeconomic status with astounding accuracy.

But a more fundamental criticism, based on the notion that all assessments are only steps on a continually changing educational landscape, is that
assessments would be more appropriate if they were based on ongoing student work, publicly accessible records, and documentation connected directly to students' classroom experiences. A number of North Dakota Study
Group monographs detail such progressive methods for student assessment.

Teaching and Curriculum

Standardized tests are integral to current school practices that increasingly
limit the autonomy of teachers, prescribing the methods they can use and
monitoring their daily practice. (Some states have even mandated specific

forms of reading instruction and outlawed others.) This approach runs counter to any progressive conception of education. It diminishes the possibility that a classroom can develop as an organic social system that supports democratic ideals. Teachers need to be able to model thinking, decision making, and flexibility in their classrooms in order to provide an intellectual and moral environment that both encourages individual growth and develops a cooperative climate. They need to be able to connect subjects in order to illustrate the relationship of school material to outside activities; and they need flexibility to incorporate the unexpected event or the students' life experiences into the curriculum.

Teachers need flexibility and autonomy to be able to attend to the growth and development of children. A rigid, inflexible curriculum and assessment system works against any possibility of a progressive education. In Dewey's words, "if the scheme . . . had been intentionally devised for relieving the teacher of the necessity of the most intimate and unremitting acquaintance with the child, nothing better could have been found" (Dewey 1906, 243).

Current federally mandated student evaluation systems—the tests of language arts, mathematics and science (starting in 2006), while ignoring all other school subjects—already have had (and will have) a devastating effect on the breadth and depth of a liberal arts curriculum. Their dominance is impoverishing the day-to-day educational work of schools and focusing teachers' and students' energies on "passing the test" rather than on learning the subjects. But, again, the major flaw from a progressive standpoint is that this focus on testing as a discrete technical activity separates it from the rest of classroom life and thus amplifies rather than diminishes the distinctions between school and the outside world. Attempts to follow a more "organic" curriculum are restricted and sharp distinctions arise between school and children's lives outside of school. As a result, many students see school activities as irrelevant to their lives.

In progressive schools, the curriculum is grounded in experiences: long-term projects; activities of the hands and mind with real materials; and, in general, tasks that are closely related to life outside the confines of school. Assessment matches the curriculum and is likely to include portfolios, detailed records, and embedded tests or quizzes. Current practice follows an opposite course: The curriculum is modified to match the tests.

Program Evaluation

At the broadest level, a progressive approach to program evaluation will require open, naturalistic evaluation methods. Recent Department of Education directives have urged educators to adopt only "scientific" research methods. By this they mean methods chosen from one particular scientific tradition—the random assignment, double-blind protocols favored for clinical medical research. The professional educational research community has challenged this idea, primarily on technical grounds: Random assignment is frequently impossible in educational settings where context is so crucial that many educational experiments require a case study approach and the relevant parameters cannot be controlled.

But again progressive principles suggest an even broader criticism: Delineation of evaluation as a circumscribed research activity separate from its social milieu requires that a host of relevant variables be eliminated. Curricula, pedagogic methods, or even student achievement are not isolated events, like a disease caused by a single agent. They are embedded in a larger sociopolitical milieu and need to be considered in that context. That is why progressive educators stress the need for flexible, holistic research methods, more akin to the work of anthropologists than that of medical researchers.

Conclusion

Dewey's writings on evaluation are scattered and less coherent than those on other aspects of education. This reflects the less-developed field of evaluation in his time when it was assumed that teachers were responsible for assessing students' progress and would match their methods to the pedagogic style they adopted.

But he is clear that considerations of evaluation, like all other aspects of education, need to adhere to the moral values of the field: They have to support the development of children and they have to reflect the need for education to support democratic values. In their effort to summarize Dewey's approach to educational evaluation, Douglas J. Simpson and Michael J. B. Jackson remind us of the following:

> Educational evaluation [according to Dewey] should focus upon both means and ends, paying particular attention to the ends of personal and social growth. The growth Dewey envisioned was a developing understanding and associated behavior that is immediately important but also enabling in the future. Whether evaluating schools and neighborhoods or teachers and students, primary attention should be given to the quality of thought, imagination, creation, communication, and behavior exhibited by individuals. These emphases set Dewey apart from most educational thinkers in his and our day and provide a framework for critiquing educational assessment and evaluation endeavors today. (2002, 419)

References

Armstrong, Michael. 1980. *Closely Observed Children: The Diary of a Primary Classroom.* London: Writers and Readers in Association with Chameleon Press.

Ashton-Warner, Sylvia. 1963. *Teacher.* New York: Simon and Schuster.

Barr, Mary A., Dana A. Craig, Delores Fisette, and Margaret A. Syverson. 1999. *Assessing, Literacy with the Learning Record: A Handbook for Teachers, Grades K–6.* Portsmouth, NH: Heinemann.

Barrs, Myra, Sue Ellis, Hilary Hester, and Anne Thomas. 1988. *Primary Language Record.* London: Inner London Education Authority/Centre for Language in Primary Education.

Bussis, Anne, and Edward Chittenden. 1970. *Analysis of an Approach to Open Education,* Project Report 70-13. Princeton: Educational Testing Service.

Bussis, Anne, Edward Chittenden, Marianne Amarel, and Edith Klausner. 1985. *Inquiry into Meaning: An Investigation of Learning to Read.* Hillsdale, NJ: Lawrence Erlbaum Associates.

Carini, Patricia. 1986. "Building from Children's Strengths." *Journal of Education* 168 (3).

———. 1994. "Framing Remarks: Stories of Experiences with Evaluation and Standards." Paper distributed at meeting of North Dakota Study Group, Woodstock, IL, February 17.

———. 2001. *Starting Strong, A Different Look at Children, Schools, and Standards.* New York: Teachers College Press.

Chittenden, Edward. 1990. "Young Children's Discussions of Science Topics." In *The Assessment of Hands-on Elementary Science Programs,* Monograph Series, North Dakota Study Group on Evaluation. Grand Forks, ND: University of North Dakota Press.

Comenius, Johann Amos. 1896. *The Great Didactic of John Amos Comenius.* Translated by W. Keatinge. London: Adam and Charles Black. (Original edition published as *Dididactica Magna, 1657.)*

Dennison, George. 1969. *The Lives of Children: The Story of the First Street School.* New York: Random House.

Dewey, John. 1897. "My Pedagogic Creed." *The School Journal* LIV (3): 77–80.

———. 1906. "Education Direct and Indirect." In *John Dewey: The Middle Works, 1899–1924,* Vol. 3, edited by Jo Ann Boydston, 240–48. Carbondale, IL: Southern Illinois University.

———. 1915. *The School and Society.* Chicago: University of Chicago Press.

———. 1931. "American Education Past and Future." In *John Dewey: The Later Works, 1925–1953,* Vol. 6, edited by Jo Ann Boydston. Carbondale IL: Southern Illinois University.

———. 1944. *Democracy and Education.* New York: The Free Press. (Original edition published in 1916. New York: Macmillan.)

———. 1956. *The Child and the Curriculum.* Chicago: University of Chicago Press.

———. 1963. *Experience and Education.* New York: MacMillan. (Original edition published in 1938. Kappa Delta Pi Publishers.)

Dewey, John, and Evelyn Dewey. 1915. *Schools of Tomorrow.* New York: E. P. Dutton.

Duckworth, Eleanor. 1996. *"The Having of Wonderful Ideas" and Other Essays on Teaching and Learning*, 2d ed. New York: Teachers College Press.

———. 2001. *Tell Me More: Listening to Learners Explain*. New York: Teachers College Press.

Engel, Brenda S. 1977. *Informal Evaluation*, Monograph Series, North Dakota Study Group on Evaluation. Grand Forks, ND: University of North Dakota Press.

———. 1995. *Considering Children's Art: Why and How to Value Their Works*. Washington, DC: National Association for the Education of Young Children.

Featherstone, Helen. 1980. *A Difference in the Family: Life with a Disabled Child*. New York: Basic Books.

Featherstone, Joseph. 1967. "Schools for Children"; "How Children Learn"; and "Teaching Children to Think." *The New Republic* (Aug. 10, Sept. 2, and Sept. 9).

———. 1971. *Schools Where Children Learn*. New York: Liveright.

———. 2002. *Dear Josie, Witnessing the Hopes and Failures of Democratic Education*. New York: Teachers College Press.

Froebel, Friedrich. 1900. *The Education of Man*. New York: Appleton. (Original English edition published in 1887.)

Hawkins, David. 1966. "Learning the Unteachable." In *Learning by Discovery: A Critical Appraisal*, edited by Lee Shulman and Evan Keislar. Chicago: Rand McNally.

———. 2002. *The Informed Vision: Essays on Learning and Human Nature*. New York: Atherton Press.

Herndon, James. 1968. *The Way It Spozed to Be*. New York: Simon and Schuster.

Himley, Margaret (ed.), with Patricia Carini. 2000. *From Another Angle: Children's Strengths and School Standards*. New York: Teachers College Press.

———. 2002. *Prospect Descriptive Processes*. North Bennington, VT: The Prospect Center.

Hoffmann, Banesh. 1962. *The Tyranny of Testing*. New York: The Crowell-Collier Press.

King, Martin Luther. 1963. *Letter from Birmingham Jail*. http://almaz.com/nobel/peace/MLK.jail.html.

———. 1968. "I've been to the Mountaintop." http://www.afscme.org/about/kingspch.htm

Klee, P. 1964. *The Diaries of Paul Klee, 1898–1918*. Berkeley: University of California Press.

Kozol, Jonathan. 1967. *Death at an Early Age*. Boston: Houghton Mifflin.

———. 1991. *Savage Inequalities: Children in America's Schools*. New York: Crown.

Linn, Susan. 2004. *Consuming Kids: The Hostile Takeover of Childhood*. New York: The New Press.

Marcon, Rebecca. 2002. "Moving Up the Grades: Relationship Between Preschool Model and Later School Success." *Early Childhood Research & Practice* 4 (1), http://ecrp.uiuc.edu/v5ni/katz.html

Marshall, Sybil. 1963. *An Experiment in Education*. Cambridge, UK: Cambridge University Press.

Mayhew, Katherine Camp, and A. C. Edwards. 1936/1965. *The Dewey School*. New York: D. Appleton-Century (1936) and Atherton Press (1965).

McDonald, Jean. 1972. "Denver National Follow Through Conference." In *Voices 1*. Newton, MA: Education Development Center.

McKinney, Alythea. 2004. Shaping History: Five Students, Three Artifacts and the Material, Social and Economic Lives of Late Nineteenth Century Butter Makers. Dissertation. Cambridge: Harvard Graduate School of Education.

Meier, Deborah. 1973. "Reading Failure and the Tests." New York: The Workshop Center for Open Education, City College of New York.

Menand, Louis. 2001. *The Metaphysical Club: A Story of Ideas in America.* New York: Farrar, Straus & Giroux.

A Nation at Risk: The Imperative for Educational Reform. 1983. Washington, DC: U.S. Government Printing Office.

National Council of Teachers of Mathematics. 1989. *Curriculum and Evaluation Standards for School Mathematics.* Reston, VA: NCTM.

———. 1991. *Professional Standards for Teaching Mathematics.* Reston, VA: NCTM.

Neill, A. S. 1960. *Summerhill.* New York City: Hart.

Paley, Vivian. 1981. *Wally's Stories.* Cambridge: Harvard University Press.

———. 1986. "On Listening to What Children Say." *Harvard Educational Review* 56 (2).

Patton, Michael Q. 1975. *Alternative Evaluation Research Paradigm,* Monograph Series, North Dakota Study Group on Evaluation. Grand Forks, ND: University of North Dakota Press.

Perrone, Vito. 1972. Opening Remarks, Meeting of North Dakota Study Group, OGL #1471. Grand Forks, ND: University of North Dakota, Orin G. Libby Manuscript Collection, Elwyn B. Robinson Department of Special Collections, Chester Fritz Library.

———. 1975. *Report to the Rockefeller Brothers Fund,* Monograph Series, North Dakota Study Group on Evaluation. Grand Forks, ND: University of North Dakota Press.

———. 1990. Dean Vito Perrone Records, UA #57. Grand Forks, ND: University of North Dakota, University Archives, Elwyn B. Robinson Department of Special Collections, Chester Fritz Library.

———. 1991a. "Large Purposes in Transforming Practice." In *Progressive Education for the 1990s.* Edited by Kathe Jervis and Carol Montag. New York: Teachers College Press.

———, ed. 1991b. *Expanding Student Assessment.* Alexandria, VA: Association for Supervison and Curriculum Development.

———. 1997. Barbara Biber Lecture, Bank St. College, September 8, 1997. Grand Forks, ND: University Archives, Elwyn B. Robinson Department of Special Collections, Chester Fritz Library.

———. 1998a. *Teacher with a Heart: Reflections on Leonard Covello and Community.* New York: Teachers College Press.

———. 1998b. Dean Vito Perrone Records. Grand Forks, ND: University Archives. Elwyn B. Robinson Department of Special Collections, Chester Fritz Library.

Perrone, Vito, and Monroe Cohen, eds. 1975. *Testing and Evaluation: New Views.* Washington, DC: Association for Childhood Education International.

Pestalozzi, Johann Heinrich. 1781. *Leonard and Gertrude.* Translated and abridged by Eva Channing, 1897: Heath & Co. Original publication in German.

———. 1801. *How Gertrude Teaches Her Children.* Translated 1898 by Lucy E. Holland and Francis C. Turner. Syracuse, NY: C. W. Bardeen. Original publication in German.

The Plowden Report. 1967. *Children and Their Primary Schools,* Vol. 1. London: Her Majesty's Stationery Office.

Prospect School Brochure. n.d. "Description of the Prospect School." North Bennington, VT: Prospect Archives and Center for Education and Research.

Public Papers of the Presidents of the United States. 1965. *Lyndon B. Johnson, 1963–64.* Vol. I, entry 357. Washington, DC: U.S. Government Printing Office.

Ramsey, Lara. 2002. "Understanding the Problem of Un-prescribing the Curriculum," paper. Cambridge: Harvard Graduate School of Education.

Reference Edition of the Prospect Archive. 1985. North Bennington, VT: The Prospect Archive and Center for Education and Research.

Roots of Open Education in America: Reminiscences and Reflections. 1976. Edited by Ruth Dropkin, with Arthur Tobier. New York: Workshop Center for Open Education at City College of New York.

Rosen, Connie, and Harold Rosen. 1973. *The Language of Primary School Children.* Harmondsworth, UK: Penguin.

Rousseau, Jean-Jacques. 1756. *The Social Contract.*

———. 1762. *Emile, or On Education.*

Sapon-Shevin, Mara. 1999. *Because We Can Change the World: A Practical Guide to Building Cooperative, Inclusive Classroom Communities.* Boston: Allyn and Bacon.

Schneier, Lisa. 1995. Apprehending Poetry: A Case Study of a Group of Six High School Students. Dissertation. Cambridge: Harvard Graduate School of Education.

Silone, Ignazio. 1949. "The God That Failed" (quoted in letter to the editor from Daniel Bell). *The New York Review of Books,* October 10, 2002.

Simpson, Douglas J., and Michael J. B. Jackson. 2002. "John Dewey and Educational Evaluation." In *Standards and Schooling in the United States,* Vol. 2, edited by Joe L. Kincheloe and Danny Weil. Santa Barbara, CA: ABC-CLIO.

Smith, Frank. 1978. *Understanding Reading: A Psycholinguistic Analysis of Reading and Learning to Read.* Hillsdale, NJ: Lawrence Erlbaum Associates.

Stewart, Heidi. 1995. "On Friday," Paper. Cambridge: Harvard Graduate School of Education.

Valdez, Guadalupe. 1996. *Con Respeto: Bridging the Distances Between Culturally Diverse Families and Schools.* New York: Teachers College Press.

Weber, Lillian. 1971. *The English Infant School and Informal Education.* Englewood Cliffs, NJ: Prentice-Hall.

Whitman, Walt. 1949. *Democratic Vistas.* New York: The Liberal Arts Press. (First published in 1871 by author as pamphlets, Washington, DC.)

Wilder, Laura Ingalls. 1935. *The Little House on the Prairie.* New York: Harper.

Williams, Raymond. 1961. *The Long Revolution.* New York: Columbia University Press.

Contributors

Vito Perrone, the original convener of the NDSG, has been a teacher, administrator, and professor of education, as well as the author of numerous books and articles.

Beth Alberty is Director of Collections at the Brooklyn Children's Museum. She was formerly on the staff of the City College of New York Workshop Center, about which she coauthored an NDSG monograph.

Ruth Dropkin, a freelance editor, was associated with Lillian Weber for more than ten years on Workshop Center publications. She also edited Weber's book, *The English Infant School and Informal Education* (1971) and, with Arthur Tobier, *The Roots of Open Education in America*, from which this book's chapter is drawn.

Joseph Featherstone, a longtime member of the NDSG, has been faculty leader of one of the teacher education programs at Michigan State University. He is the author of many books and articles including, most recently, *Dear Josie, Witnessing the Hopes and Failures of Democratic Education* (TC Press, 2002).

Alice Seletsky taught elementary school in New York City for more than thirty-five years. Her postretirement activities include volunteer work at Central Park East school and at the Museum of Natural History.

Edith Klausner is retired from a busy life of teaching, researching, administration, and educational consulting. She collaborated with Educational Testing Service researchers and the Philadelphia school district teachers on a book about children learning to read.

Harold Berlak writes about curriculum, educational assessment, and educational policy. He is an independent researcher; a fellow at the Educational Policy Research Unit at Arizona State University; and a senior research fellow at the Applied Research Center, Oakland, California.

Francisco Guajardo taught at Edcouch-Elsa High School throughout the 1990s, founded the Llano Grande Center for Research and Development, and is assistant professor of Educational Leadership at the University of Texas–Pan American in Edinburg, Texas.

Hollee Freeman, a former elementary teacher, is currently working as a senior research and development specialist at TERC. She is also working on her dissertation in the field of educational administration at Boston College.

Connie Henry has been an educator for thirty years in a variety of settings and roles. She is the assistant director at the Atrium School in Watertown, Massachusetts. Currently, she is writing a book about her school's approach to teaching and learning.

Kathe Jervis is a longtime teacher, educational researcher, and is now coordinator of Columbia Urban Educators (CUE), a program supporting Columbia graduates who teach in New York City public schools.

Joseph H. Suina is a professor of teacher education for elementary schools, director of the Institute for American Indian Education, and tribal leaders' liaison person for the Office of the Provost at the University of New Mexico.

186

Mara Sapon-Shevin is professor of Inclusive Education at Syracuse University. Her areas of interest include teaching for social justice, teacher education, and using music and dance to build community and teach for justice. Her most recent book is *Because We Can Change the World: A Practical Guide for Building Cooperative, Inclusive Classroom Communities.*

Louisa Cruz-Acosta has taught young children in New York City public elementary schools, including a small, progressive alternative school she cofounded, for the past sixteen years. She also worked with incarcerated adolescents and their families in New York State residential facilities for eight years.

Anne C. Martin, now retired, taught in public elementary schools for more than thirty years. She has published numerous articles and is the author of an NDSG monograph and is also the assistant editor of this book.

Rebecca E. Dyasi is a science education professor at Long Island University in Brooklyn, New York, and conducts teacher professional development programs for the New York City school district. Prior to becoming a professor, she taught in elementary and high schools for eighteen years.

Hubert M. Dyasi is professor at the City College of the City University of New York. He has directed education development programs in New York, nationally, and overseas. He has also participated in numerous North Dakota Study Group activities and contributed to one of its monographs.

Brenda S. Engel has been an art teacher, consultant on Open Education, and program evaluator. Now retired from teaching at Lesley University, she has published articles and monographs and is the editor of this book.

Deborah Meier has worked in New York City and Boston public schools for forty years. She founded and was principal of Central Park East and Mission Hill schools. Since her early days as a kindergarten teacher she has written for, and been actively involved in, the NDSG.

Helen Featherstone, who currently teaches teachers, prospective teachers, and doctoral students at Michigan State University, is the author of *A Difference in the Family: Life with a Disabled Child* and the founding editor of the *Harvard Education Letter* and *Changing Minds,* a bulletin on school reform.

Diane K. Mullins taught in the New York City public schools for more than thirty years. Her informal classroom has been a site for teacher preparation, documentation, research, and publication.

Eleanor Duckworth, a member of the Harvard Graduate School of Education faculty, focuses on questions of how people learn things and what anybody else can do to help.

Leslie Alexander has worked in public schools for more than thirty years. She is currently the principal of the Six to Six Inter-district Magnet School in Bridgeport, Connecticut.

Rhoda Kanevsky, recently retired from the Philadelphia public schools after teaching young children for more than thirty years, is a founding member of the Philadelphia Teachers' Learning Cooperative. She presently teaches in the Reading, Writing, and Literacy Program at the Graduate School of Education, UPenn.

Lynne Strieb, a retired teacher, is a founding member of the Philadelphia Teachers' Learning Cooperative. She taught in the Philadelphia public schools for thirty-one years and is the author of several published essays and of an NDSG monograph.

Betsy Wice works as a reading teacher at the Frederick Douglass Elementary School in North Philadelphia.

Edward (Ted) Chittenden is a developmental psychologist who has investigated classroom-based methods for documenting and understanding children's learning.

Susan Harman is a charter school principal in California and has been an educator and author for thirty-five years, as well as an organizer for her entire life.

Patricia F. Carini is a cofounder of the Prospect School (1965–1991) and the Prospect Archives and Center for Education and Research (1979–present).

George E. Hein, a Lesley University professor emeritus, is a founding member of the North Dakota Study Group on Evaluation. He has written extensively on student assessment and on learning in museums.

North Dakota
Study Group Monographs*

Carini, Patricia F. 1975, Feb. *Observation and Description: An Alternative Methodology for the Investigation of Human Phenomena.*

By the former director of the Prospect Archive and Center for Evaluation and Research, North Bennington, Vermont. Carini contends "that the model approach to school reform has inherent weaknesses and, further, that the continued vitality and evolution of far-reaching reform movements such as the progressive movement and its latter day derivative, informal (open) education, depend upon the articulation of a methodology, congruent with their philosophical orientation, that will explicate and validate their undertaking."

Cook, Ann, and Deborah Meier. n.d.. *Reading Tests: Do They Help or Hurt Your Child?*

A booklet directed at parents that is intended to inform them about the contents and effects of standardized tests on children and schools. The authors illustrate their point of view with test questions "typical of those found on the usual commercial standardized reading tests."

Cook, Ann, and Deborah Meier. 1975, Feb. *Reading Tests: What Does That Score Mean?*

A companion booklet to the authors' previous one on reading tests, this publication explains for laypeople how scores on standardized tests are determined.

Engel, Brenda S. 1975, Feb. *A Handbook on Documentation.*

"A systematic documentation is designed to reflect a complicated, many-faceted sequence of events that has occurred over a period of time so that it may be examined at leisure. . . . These kinds of records can be classified into two general types: those that represent samples or illustrations (of work, of an activity, etc.) and those that sum up a situation or aspects of a program."

*Feiman, Sharon. 1975, Feb. *Teacher Curriculum Work Center: A Descriptive Study.*

"This is a story about how a group of teachers started a teacher center [which opened in October 1972 in a YMCA on Chicago's south side]."

Hein, George E. 1975, Feb. *An Open Education Perspective on Evaluation.*

Using the then current language of "open education," Hein spells out the progressive position on both assessment and evaluation—that is, on evaluative judgments of children and programs.

---

*This list was collated by Monroe D. Cohen. All titles are in chronological order by original date of publication. Quotations are from the monographs' introductions. Only titles marked with an asterisk are currently in print.

Patton, Michael Quinn. 1975, Feb. *Alternative Evaluation Research Paradigms.*
"I have outlined two paradigms of evaluation research. To facilitate analysis and discussion, I have looked at these paradigms through a set of dichotomies: qualitative versus quantitative methodology, validity versus reliability, subjectivity versus objectivity, closeness to versus distance from the data, holistic versus component analysis, process versus outcome evaluation. . . . Neither paradigm can meet all evaluation needs."

Cook, Ann, and Herb Mack. 1975, Dec. *The Word and the Thing: Ways of Seeing the Teacher.*
By the codirectors of the Community Resources Institute in New York City. Subtitled "a statement regarding teacher education, teacher accountability, and the teacher as researcher." Among the significant topics of inquiry was consideration of the connections between children's and teachers' behavior.

Harlow, Steven D. 1975, Dec. *Special Education: The Meeting of Differences.*
The tone of the essay is critical of many of the practices of the special education profession.

Perrone, Vito. 1975, Dec. *A Report to the Rockefeller Brothers Fund.*
A summary of the activities of the North Dakota Study Group in 1975 and an outline of its directions for the year ahead (1976) by its convener and coordinator, then dean of the Center for Teaching and Learning, University of North Dakota, Grand Forks. Appendices include a list of participants and of the materials forwarded to them from May 1973 to May 1975.

Horwitz, Robert A. 1976, June. *Psychological Effects of Open Classroom Teaching on Primary School Children: A Review of the Research.*
A comprehensive survey of evaluative research (of "progressive" practice from 1939 to the 1950s and of more recent "open" schools in the United States, Canada, and England). "While the summative evaluation on open classrooms is inconclusive, there is a great demand for continuing formative evaluation, aimed at, in Carini's words, 'providing an ever more responsive setting for children.'"

Elliott, John. 1976, Sept. *Developing Hypotheses About Classrooms from Teachers' Practical Constructs.*
"Reformers have largely failed to realize that fundamental changes in classroom practice can only be brought about if teachers become conscious of the theories, which guide their practice, and are able to reflect critically about them." This action-research involved forty teachers from twelve schools.

Williams, John D. 1976, Sept. *Testing and the Testing Industry: A Third View.*
"The debate regarding standardized testing in general, and intelligence testing in particular, has quietly risen to a commanding position on the agenda of all those parties trying to influence the policy of American education. . . . Perhaps a most useful solution to the testing problem [a Third View] is the construction of criterion-referenced work samples."

Olson, Paul. 1976, Dec. *A View of Power: Four Essays on the National Assessment of Educational Progress.*

"I wish to argue that the National Assessment of Educational Progress, in its power base, conception, creation, and execution runs against what I have described as the court view and supports what I have called the professional view."

*Rayder, Nick, ed. 1977, Feb. *First California Conference on Educational Evaluation and Public Policy.*

Reports on a 1976 conference of representatives of groups involved in educational evaluation in the San Francisco Bay Area.

*Churchill, Edith, and Joseph Petner Jr. 1977, Mar. *Children's Language and Thinking: A Report of Work-in-Progress.*

"Represents an effort to critically examine and reflect upon a year's exploration in the use of children's language—observed, recorded, and analyzed in a K–1 Bank Street College Follow Through site—as a basis for staff development."

Engel, Brenda S. 1977, Mar. *Informal Evaluation.*

"This monograph is intended to complement *A Handbook of Evaluation* [which was] published in 1975. The general purpose . . . is to explore new and more reasonable ways of assessing children's learning; the narrower purpose of these two monographs is to suggest some specific, practical evaluation methods for people without special knowledge or expertise in evaluation who are concerned with elementary education."

Ross, Sylvia, Herbert Zimiles, and David Gerstein. 1977, Dec. *Children's Interactions in Traditional and Nontraditional Classrooms.*

A shortened version of a 1975 report submitted to the Ford Foundation by researchers of the Bank Street College of Education in New York City. "[It] presents the results of a comparative study of group interaction in contrasting educational environments with children of different socioeconomic backgrounds."

Duckworth, Eleanor. 1978, Feb. *The African Primary Science Program: An Evaluation and Extended Thoughts.*

At the time of its writing, Eleanor Duckworth was a teacher at the Faculté de Psychologie et des Sciences de l'Education, University of Geneva. "This monograph is cast primarily in the form of a research report, but it is much more than that. My principal purpose . . . is to alert readers to the importance of attending not only to the findings but [also] to the way of thinking about evaluation that guided the inquiry."

Hull, Bill. 1978, Apr. *Teachers' Seminars on Children's Thinking: A Progress Report.*

The author describes himself as "a former teacher who continues to have a strong interest in the study of thinking. . . . After six years of successful seminaring [about children's thinking, by experienced teachers], we are convinced that there are strong advantages in sharing specifics with people who are immersed in rich experiencing with children, in bringing different points of view to bear on the same evidence, in making note of the formulations that grow out of our sharing, and [in] using these formulations . . . to help us see more clearly."

Jervis, Kathe. 1978, Sept. *Children's Thinking in the Classroom.*

A participant for several years in Bill Hull's seminar on children's thinking in Cambridge, Massachusetts, the author led a seminar of her own in Los Angeles. "The seminar was a source of support as well as the start of a powerful process of growth.

Many teachers have a difficult time understanding and accepting such an open-ended enterprise as I had in my classroom; before the seminar, I was one of those teachers."

*Carini, Patricia F. 1979, Sept. *The Art of Seeing and the Visibility of the Person.*
This monograph "schematizes a metaphysics of observing, and presents a method of gathering and organizing empirical observations in order to disclose meaning."

Olson, Ruth Anne. 1980, Dec. *Evaluation as Interaction in Support of Change.*
Describes how an independent evaluator worked with special education teachers at Marcy School in Minneapolis Minnesota. "Traditionally we see teachers as being the people who teach and evaluators as the people who watch the teaching. Learning does not acknowledge such dichotomies. Schools should make evaluation a shared learning experience."

*Kinghorn, Norton D., Lester Faigley, and Thomas Clemens. 1981, May. *A Syntactic Approach to College Writing.*
This is a report on two studies of pedagogical research about holistic evaluation done at the University of North Dakota. "[It] . . . examines Francis Christensen's theory of generative rhetoric, both as a rhetorical theory and as a method of teaching college writing."

Alberty, Beth, James Neujahr, and Lillian Weber. 1981, Nov. *Use and Setting: Development in a Teachers' Center.*
At the time of its writing, Lillian Weber was director of the Workshop Center of the City University of New York and a professor at the College's School of Education (as was associate dean James Neujahr). Beth Alberty was a documenter and researcher at the Workshop Center and at the Prospect Center in North Bennington, Vermont. This is a historical and evaluative report. "Use and setting at the Workshop Center were documented for the study through observations, questionnaires, interviews, and perusal of the Center's records."

*Carini, Patricia F. 1982, Aug. *The School Lives of Seven Children: A Five-Year Study.*
A report based on data from an evaluation of the New York Experimental Prekindergarten under the leadership of Ruth Flurry.

Buxton, Amity. 1982, Sept. *Further Dimensions of Assessing Language Development.*
Basing her work on developmental theory, Buxton presents a "way of looking at young children's writing by setting forth dimensions for analyzing and assessing their spontaneous writing (and drawing) in daily journals."

Martin, Anne. 1982, Nov. *The Words in My Pencil: Considering Children's Writing.*
This monograph is an exploration of ways of eliciting writing from children. "What I have written is not a how-to book. All teachers have to work out their own approaches from a variety of sources outside themselves. But there are insights I have reached through ordinary trial-and-error groping in the classroom which may be helpful to other teachers."

Rosen, Connie. 1983, Sept. *What About Children Who Can't?: On Writing.*
By the director of a two-year project, Language Development in the Primary School, which was initiated by the English Committee of the School Council (of England).

This essay is taken from the book *The Language of Primary School Children*, one of the major outcomes of the project.

*Apelman, Maja, David Hawkins, and Philip Morrison. 1985, Feb. *Critical Barriers Phenomenon in Elementary Science.*

David Hawkins was professor of philosophy at the University of Colorado, Boulder, where he was director of the Mountain View Center for Environmental Education from 1970 to 1982. Maja Apelman was a staff member at the Center, and Philip Morrison a physicist at MIT. The essays in this monograph (except Morrison's) were adapted from material published elsewhere as research reports or journal articles.

Barritt, Loren, Ton Beekman, Hans Bleeker, and Karel Mulderij. 1985, Sept. *Researching Educational Practice.*

Loren Barritt, professor of education at the University of Michigan, went as a Fulbright lecturer to Utrecht, Holland, where he met Ton Beekman who was a professor at the Pedagogical Institute at the University there. Bleeker and Mulderij were students of Beekman in Holland. "This monograph is not another research recipe book. Of research recipes we have had enough! . . . We have only addressed the issues that we thought we needed to discuss to make clear why we have opted for phenomenology and why you should feel free to do so as well."

Strieb, Lynne. 1985, Sept. *A (Philadelphia) Teacher's Journal.*

A veteran early childhood teacher shares parts of her school journal—"a narrative record of class discussions to augment the daily notes and records of individual children"—which she has kept since she began teaching in 1972. Also included are "reflections and questions that emerged, through books, and through associations with colleagues in the Philadelphia Teachers' Learning Cooperative and at the Prospect Summer Institutes."

Boston Women's Teachers' Group: Sara Freedman, Jane Jackson, and Katherine Boles. 1986, Feb. *The Effect of Teaching on Teachers.*

An edited version of a report to the National Institute of Education. The research project investigates the effects of the institutional structures of schools on the teaching of female elementary school teachers. "We focused on twenty-five subjects who substantially matched the national teacher population in terms of socioeconomic and racial background, marital status, educational attainment of parents, and father's occupations imposed by such a small sample. . . . Altogether 219 hours of interviewing time were logged."

Yeomans, Edward. 1986, Feb. *When the Voice of the Teacher Is Heard in the Land.*

By the former headmaster of Shady Hill School in Cambridge, Massachusetts, it contains a capsule history of the Progressive Education Movement in the United States. Also includes excerpts by Lillian Weber from her book *The English Infant School and Informal Education* and by Adelaide Sproul from *An Advisor's Notebook.*

*Traugh, Cecelia, Rhoda Kanevsky, Anne Martin, Alice Seletsky, Karen Woolf, and Lynne Strieb. 1986, Oct. *Speaking Out: Teachers on Teaching.*

"Voices" of six experienced teachers from Philadelphia, New York City, and Brookline and Wenham, Massachusetts, who share accounts of "our teaching practice—what it is and what it could be. It is about teachers—what we do and how we think about and learn from what is done."

Duckworth, Eleanor. 1986, Nov. *Inventing Density.*

"This is a story about the collective creation of knowledge" in eight weekly sessions of a course in educational psychology where "students find out something for themselves, through their own investigations of everyday phenomena, and then draw psychological and pedagogical themes from this joint engagement."

Engel, Brenda S. 1987, Nov. *Between Feeling and Fact.*

This monograph sought "to collect and look with care at work by children below high school age [that] had some reference to the subject of nuclear war—pictures, writings, and, if possible, recorded discussions—to see what they suggested about the children's thoughts and feelings."

*Kallick, Bena. 1989, Dec. *Changing Schools into Communities for Thinking.*

Presents a vision of what a truly educational classroom community might look like, "one where the active process of interpretation is used to give meaning to learning that is taking place."

Hein, George E., ed. 1990, Aug. *The Assessment of Hands-On Elementary Science Programs.*

A collection of articles on the theory and practice of science assessment. The outcome of an NSF-supported conference, the articles are by experts in the fields of both assessment and science education; several of them are members of the North Dakota Study Group.

*Hall, Lynne, Lynn Stuart, and Brenda S. Engel, eds. 1995, Feb. *The Cambridge Handbook of Documentation and Assessment: Child Portfolios and Teacher Records in the Primary Grades.*

This handbook is "intended to support and guide teachers' use of portfolios rather than testing for purposes of assessing student progress." It contains many examples of relevant forms and records taken from actual classroom use.

*Kallet, Tony. 1995, Feb. *Few Adults Crawl: Thoughts on Young Children Learning.*

A posthumously published collection of writings taken from articles and memoranda Kallet produced while working for the Leicestershire Education Authority in England. Kallet's singularly imaginative, penetrating insights were edited by his friends and colleagues Bill Browse and Mary Brown.

Dyasi, Hubert (Introduction), Lillian Weber, Olga Winbush, Joseph Suina, Ruth Anne Olson, and Arthur Tobier. 1996, Mar. *Valuing Each Other: Perspectives on Culturally Responsive Teaching.*

Five essays, with preface by editor Monroe D. Cohen, on ways to respond to the need for cultural understanding and responsiveness. Hubert Dyasi was the successor to Lillian Weber as director of the City College Workshop Center. Citing his own experiences growing up in apartheid South Africa, he says: "In the face of a bleak picture of wholesome multiculturist practices, [these essays] paint a landscape of possibility and of the constructive role that schools can play in its realization."

Index